A Fountain of Language Development for Early Childhood Education and the Special Child, Too

A FOUNTAIN OF LANGUAGE DEVELOPMENT FOR EARLY CHILDHOOD EDUCATION AND THE SPECIAL CHILD, TOO

Leola G. Hayes, Ph.D.

Illustrated by Virginia Snedeker Taylor

VANTAGE PRESS
NEW YORK

The author wishes to acknowledge permission to reprint the following:

Poems from *Finger Frolics—Fingerplays for Young Children* (Michigan: Partner Press, 1983):

"Ten Little Fingers"
"Five Little Squirrels"
"Open, Shut Them"
"Snowflakes"
"The Eency, Weency Spider"

The Christmas Santa Almost Missed (Mahwah, NJ: Troll Associates, Inc.)
He's Got the Whole World in His Hands by Tom Glaser (New York: Doubleday)
"The Search" by Dr. Alice Meeker

FIRST EDITION

Copyright © 1991 by Leola G. Hayes, Ph.D.

Published by Vantage Press, Inc.
516 West 34th Street, New York, New York 10001

Manufactured in the United States of America
ISBN: 0-533-08911-5

Library of Congress Catalog Card No.: 90-90004

0 9 8 7 6 5 4 3 2 1

To
Spurgeon S. Hayes, my husband,
and
Dora H. Hayes, my aunt,
for their patience, sensitivity, understanding, and enthusiasm

To
the late Dr. Alice M. Meeker
(former professor at William Paterson College)

Contents

Part IV. Choral Speaking

Foreword

This book, *A Fountain of Language Development for Early Childhood Education and the Special Child, Too,* contains material for six basic areas in the education of pre-schoolers. This volume will develop the verbal ability and communication skills for the pre-school child.

The six areas can each enrich the child's vocabulary and stimulate his use of language. The areas dealt with in the book are:

- Stories
- Finger plays
- Poems
- Choral speaking
- Number readiness
- Singing Activities

A picture file collected by the classroom teacher is an invaluable teaching source.

Stories:

The storyteller refreshes the weary, rejoices the sad and multiplies the joy of those who are already glad.

—Cynthia Maus

A pre-school child who hears stories told and demonstrated each day builds word pictures in his head. Later on, he will recall these stories and retell them to his peers and family. Next, he will begin to create short stories to amuse his friends. Stories are a gift to every young child.

Finger plays are an ever present source of language development. Each child has his ten fingers ready to follow the teacher's verse:

This is the church
This is the steeple
Open up and see the people.

Many finger plays give a variety of language terms. Then the children will put up two or three fingers and relate something about to happen. Thus the author has brought in number concepts. Also, there is some creative activity.

Poems: The teacher of pre-school or other young children will know many poems and use them as a way of introducing something new. Young children are fascinated by holidays and their symbols. A short poem about a turkey (see "First of All You Trace a Nickel") makes Thanksgiving meaningful to a three- or four-year-old. A poem about a jack-o'-lantern with big cut-out eyes and mouth makes Halloween a special day for young children.

Choral Speaking: In every group of children we will find children who like to perform, but not alone (the shy child). Choral speaking provides reciting together. These children enjoy reciting short poems or verses with a group. It gives them courage, security, unity, and the experience of being a part of the group. These children learn listening skills and following directions. They know exactly when to start and finish with their classmates.

Number readiness and rhymes are the beginning of a listening experience for pre-schoolers. The teacher introduces the rhymes and calls attention to the *end* words: "Listen for words that rhyme."

Little Bo Peep
Has lost her ———
And can't tell where to find them.
Leave them alone
And they'll come ———
Wagging their tails
Behind them.

This language-based Resource Guide offers a strong foundation for pre-school handicapped children.

A brief sketch of Dr. Hayes' background explains why she is so well equipped to write in this area.

Dr. Leola G. Hayes has taught young children from pre-school age through the elementary grades. Before becoming a college professor, she was supervisor of young children from pre-school through high school.

Dr. Hayes is well known for workshops, which she has presented in the United States and abroad. Her methods of training parents of young children are much in demand.

She is the author of two previous books titled: *Come and Get It: Reading Made Easy for Reluctant Readers*, and *I Can Help the Teacher: A Program in Training for the Non-Academic Teacher Aide*.

Dr. Alice M. Meeker*
Professor Emeritus
William Paterson College
Wayne, New Jersey

*Dr. Meeker passed away on October 24, 1987.

Introduction

The period of early childhood sees the emergence of persistent patterns of emotional behavior, specific learning disabilities, sensory disorders, speech and language disorders, and subaverage general intellectual functioning. As parents and teachers of the pre-school special needs child, we are interested in good beginnings for our children.

Although the social significance of special education is now generally recognized, our society still lags behind in its recognition of great changes in abilities and behavior which take place in the pre-school special needs child.

The right start in the early years is an invaluable aid for the continuous unfolding or developing of the child's potential. The pre-school experience gives the child his first real acquaintance with the community, living beyond the familiar range of daily life in the family.

These early years may well prove to be the most fruitful for the special needs child's education, which should give him a start into the future. During these trying times bitterness, abuse, and neglect, we should get on with the job with an early and profitable beginning for all young children.

This guide is meant to be a mixture of ideas and ideals; one must complement the other. As teachers, our business is children and, here, pre-school children. Part of this "swift and solemn transition of life" passes through our hand; here we find the adults of tomorrow. As the adults become, so will be our nation in a complex and demanding society.

Pre-school teaching is the basis of all teaching in the same way that first grade reading underlies upper grade reading. Reading is a specific subject with tangible goals that can be measured by testing, but pre-school teaching has no gauge by which it can be measured, for it involves affection and responsibility and building of trust and self-esteem. That's why a teacher cannot be replaced by either a teaching machine or a computer.

A teacher's affection for her class sets the climate, and the children respond accordingly. If she is a firm, wise, and loving human being, her pupils will be relaxed and happy. Add teaching techniques and ingenuity to such a person, and you will have almost an ideal. But take away that warmth of personality and the little sympathetic extras that are never found in an educational textbook, and you have only efficiency. It's a little like the difference between a steam radiator and an open fireplace: both give out heat, but a fireplace lends more charm to the room. Ideally, the room would be more comfortable if it had both; neither is quite adequate alone.

Affection involves individuals and the constant interplay of personalities. But in a classroom responsibility belongs to the teacher—legally, to be sure, but also in a moral sense. Three- and four-year-olds are too young to have ideals of their own; a child's thinking reflects the thinking of adults, and he is exposed to his teacher between thirty and sixty hours per week.

The teacher knows that the three- to-seven-year-old pupil is just a young child. She knows that this child has few yesterdays to draw upon and small concern for tomorrow. We must understand that this is the child's first great experience away from his family. Therefore, every day is a new adventure; yet it is today that matters, and it is today upon which the teacher must build new bonds for learning. Teaching is not easy, if it is done well. But teachers must learn to anticipate the needs of themselves as well as the needs of the class. Thus confidence will be gained, and confidence is the memory of past experiences.

Contrary to popular opinion and wishful thinking, every teacher should plan carefully what she is going to teach and how the material is going to be taught before getting up in front of a class. In one sense, pupils are quite helpless. They must do what the teacher wants them to do, and their learning depends on the teacher's skills. If the teacher knows what she is doing, then she has purpose in her teaching and the children will benefit. An efficient teacher is a long-range planner. She would never take a trip of any distance without knowing her destination and the points along the way. Confucius has said that the best way to begin a journey of five thousand miles is to take the first step.

In reviewing many programs throughout the country and abroad, I have found probably the most significant, promising, and far-reaching change for the three- and four-year level related to a reorganization of a school and/or a classroom or center is the promotion of individualized learning. This organization, logically carried out, reaches every aspect of the curriculum—the teacher, the motivations for learning, and, necessarily, what is learned. In the development of an individualized curriculum, the teacher gets to make eye-to-eye contact with each child and gets the opportunity to sit with each child and bodily support each one's decision and, as young children will say, "She is my teacher all to myself." Young children need that feeling of being "a part of," belonging, "attention for me," and building bonds. An individualized program not only provides individualized instruction for each child, but gives the child the experience of being talked to, sought out, and cuddled, all of which strengthen the child's ego.

Dr. Martin Deutch directed an experimental classroom for the Institute of Developmental Studies at New York University. The aim was to develop in the early years those areas most functional and operative in the school situation, thus reducing school failure and increasing school success. Skills contributing to this goal are considered to be "the visual and auditory perception that underlies reading, language abilities, spatial and temporal orientation, general information, familiarity with books, toys, games, imagination, and the development of a sustained curiosity." Basically, the program implies that achievement depends upon precise input.

For many years now there has been a desire to "simplify" things for young children. We seem to talk a lot about moving from the simple to the complex. Do we actually know what is simple for a child? Does it mean small units? Does it mean by way of "Task Analysis"? Traditionally, each move was from one area to the next according to the child's wishes. Maybe this was good, but so many children need someone to guide them individually, explain, demonstrate, and direct their every step for security purposes. Again, the aim is to reduce school failure and increase school success.

Let us now turn our attention to the curriculum for young children. Almost all of the programs developing in the three-to-seven age range vary tremendously in scope. Some take a behaviorist approach, some are multi-dimensional, some narrowly single-dimensional, and still others include in their approach all the psychodynamics of growth and learning and seem to carry out in spirit individual concerns for all children.

A classroom is a small but potent autocracy in which children follow directions and fall under the approval or disapproval of the teacher. How that teacher thinks is important.

This sense of moral responsibility helps a teacher make the decision between what is essential and what is relatively unimportant. During the pre-school years, this may encompass the gradual development of social skills, personal habits of cleanliness, fine and gross motor skills, communication skills, reading readiness skills, and number readiness skills. In these areas, the young schoolchildren are quiet—they see; they listen; they select. The teacher has a great deal to do with the shaping of tomorrow's society.

Basic as these concepts are, they are not sufficient. Teaching young children demands knowledge and skill. There are good, honest tricks in any trade, and any teacher worthy of the name needs a whole big bagful. Skills for young children are refined and developed up through the second and third grades.

Teaching has a lifelong effect on the average child. Effective teaching is a combination of idealism and practicality in which laughter and affection go hand in hand with control and competence. It is a complex job that looks deceptively simple to the average eye, and, much like other situations, is only as good as the person who guides it. In this situation that person is the teacher. "There stands the teacher on stage."

The teacher of young children has the good common sense and proper insight to worry about tomorrow. She does her thinking ahead of time and always with the child in mind. She plans for June in September and patiently plots her days toward the ultimate goals of learning. She is fully aware that learning means making changes in the child and modifying each day's educational experiences.

It is felt that this book should be used by classroom teachers, adapted physical education specialists, and parents. Families could find a great deal of enjoyment from singing, playing, and looking with their children.

All materials used here were tested in various classrooms on young children. All activities had to be simple, clear, adaptable, and repetitive in many classroom situations. The activities were chosen due to their popularity.

The format used in this book is simple throughout. You will find in part 1 information for both teacher and parent—information on parent participation and ways in which parents can help both the teacher and child. We know that young children learn in a variety of ways; therefore, we must consider each child's learning style. In the succeeding parts you will find many tasks to be performed by the children, materials that are required, and benefits to be achieved.

It is the author's hope that you will enjoy as many hours of fun using this book as she did in assembling the many activities.

(Unless otherwise indicated, the authors of the poems included are unknown.)

A Fountain of Language Development
for Early Childhood Education and
the Special Child, Too

Part I
Number Awareness

Introduction

Objectives

The children will develop an awareness of shapes, sizes, positioning, comparison, and sets and the ability to recognize a one-to-one concept: as many as, larger than, the same as. Vocabulary will also increase.

Benefits

- Visual and auditory skills
- Coordination skills
- Development of concentration skills
- Use of voice dynamics
- Finger dexterity
- Number recognition
- Opportunity for dramatic play
- Attention building
- Practice in arithmetic skills
- Exposure to counting "without numbers"
- Listening skills
- Gentle humor
- Speech and language skills

The games in the following sections are examples of arithmetic readiness activities in the strands of *number recognition, set recognition, positioning, counting, numeration,* and *comparison.*

Pre-number and number activities provide a foundation for developing number concepts. Recognizing one-to-one leads to the concept of as many as, which is the first step toward understanding numbers.

The positioning activities provide experience with positional ideas such as over and under, top and bottom, and in front of and behind. These activities are important to a child's understanding of his environment as well as an aid to him in his ability to follow directions.

Children learn to compare things in the environment according to size. They develop an awareness of not only how two things compare, but how several things compare. They learn to observe the answers to comparison questions. Vocabulary will be increased with the use of terms such as *lighter* and *lightest, heavier* and *heaviest, more* and *most, smaller* and *smallest, longer* and *longest,* and *larger* and *largest.*

3

Number Readiness Activities

Adam Had Seven Sons

Adam had seven sons, seven sons had Adam, and they all were bright and gay, and they did what Adam did say. "Let's all do this, let's all do this," says Adam.

(Can be played as a circle game, with Adam in the center. At "Let's all do this," Adam makes any sort of motion he wishes and the circle imitates him. I believe it would be more effective if only seven sons were allowed in each circle.)

Who Built the Ark? Noah, Noah*

Refrain:
Who built the ark? Noah, Noah. Who built the ark? Brother Noah built the ark.
Stanzas:
Sing 1, 2, 3, and 4, then turn to refrain.
1. Now didn't old Noah build the ark? Built it out of hickory bark.
2. He built it long, both wide and tall. Plenty of room for the large and small.
3. He found him an axe, and hammer too. Began to cut and began to hew.
4. And every time that hammer did ring, Noah shout and Noah sing.
Refrain:
10. Now in come the animals seven by seven, four from home and the rest from heaven.
11. Now in come the animals eight by eight, some were on time and others were late.
12. Now in come the animals nine by nine, some was a-shoutin' and some was a-cryin'.
13. Now in come the animals ten by ten, five black roosters and five black hens.
14. Now Noah says, "Go shut that door. The rain's started dropping, and we can't take more."
Refrain

*From *American Folk Songs for Children*, by R. C. Seeger.

Eight Pigs

Two mother pigs lived in a pen.
Each had four babies and that made ten.
These four babies were black and white.
These four babies were black as night.
All eight babies loved to play.
And they rolled and they rolled in the mud all day.

Two Little Blackbirds

Two little blackbirds
Sitting on a hill,
One named Jack,
And the other named Jill.

Fly away, Jack,
Fly away, Jill.

Come back, Jack,
Come back, Jill.

The Tall Snowmen

One snowman standing tall,
One more snowman came to call.
Two snowmen standing tall,
One more snowman came to call.
Three snowmen standing tall,
One more snowman came to call.
Four snowmen standing tall,
One more snowman came to call.
Five snowmen standing tall,
One more snowman came to call.
Six snowmen standing tall,
One more snowman came to call.
Seven snowmen standing tall,
One more snowman came to call.
Eight snowmen standing tall,
One more snowman came to call.
Nine snowmen standing tall,
One more snowman came to call.
Ten snowmen standing tall.

Five Little Frisky Frogs

Five little frisky frogs
Hopping on the shore
One hopped into the pond
SPLASH
So then there were just four.

Four little frisky frogs
Climbing up a tree
One fell into the grass
BOOM
So then there were just three.

Three little frisky frogs
Bathing in the dew
One caught a sneezy cold
AHCHOO
So then there were just two.

Two little frisky frogs
Sleeping in the sun
One slept the day away
SNORE
So then there was just one.

One little frisky frog
Sitting on a stone
Let's call his four friends back
YOO-HOO
So he won't be alone.

Finger Plays—Number Concepts

By'm Bye

By'm bye, by'm bye, stars shining.
Number, number one, number two, number three.
Good Lawd, by'm bye, by'm bye.
Good Lawd, by'm bye.

(Finger Play: Number one, et cetera: continue up to five or ten. Many objects can be counted, such as buttons, children, windows, or foolish things like untied shoes.)
(Tone Play: Children echo "By'm bye" without being asked and like to join in on the numbering phrases.)

Over in the Meadow*

Over in the meadow in the sand, in the sun,
Lived a little mother frog and her little froggie one
"Croak," said the mother. "I croak," said the one
So they croaked and were glad in the sand, in the sun.

Over in the meadow in a pond so blue
Lived an old mother duck and her little ducks two
"Quack," said the mother. "We quack," said the two
So they quacked and were glad in the pond so blue.

Over in the meadow in a hole in the tree
Lived an old mother bluebird and her little birdies three
"Tweet," said the mother. "We tweet," said the three
So they sang and were glad in the hole in the tree.

Over in the meadow on a rock by the shore
Lived an old mother snake and her little snakes four
"Hiss," said the mother. "We hiss," said the four
So they hissed and were glad on the rock by the shore.

Over in the meadow in a big bee hive
Lived an old mother bee and her little bees five.
"Buzz," said the mother. "We buzz," said the five
So they buzzed and were glad in the big bee hive.

*From *The Fireside Book of Children's Songs*, collected by Marie Winn (New York: Simon and Schuster, 1966).

Six Little Ducks

Goals: To memorize the counting verse and learn the concepts of fat and little and to learn the concept of how some animals talk or the sounds they make.

Six little ducks that I once knew,
Fat ducks and little ducks too.
But the one little duck with the feather on his back,
He led the others with a quack, quack, quack.
Quack, quack, quack, quack, quack, quack,
He led the others with a quack, quack, quack.
Down to the meadow they would go,
Wiggle wag, wiggle wag, to and fro.
But the other little duck with the feather on his back,
He led the others with a quack, quack, quack.

Ten Little Fingers

Goal: To teach the concepts of down and out.

Ten little fingers
Sleeping in a row
Ding-dong goes the bell
And down the pole they go.

Off on the engine
Oh, oh, oh
Using the big hose
So, so, so.

When all the fire's out
Home so, so
Back in the bed
All in a row.

Put Your Finger in the Air

Put one finger in the air, in the air
Put one finger in the air, in the air
Put one finger in the air, and leave it about a year
Put one finger in the air, in the air.

Put two fingers on your head, on your head
Put two fingers on your head, on your head
Put two fingers on your head, tell me is it green or red
Put two fingers on your head, on your head.

Put three fingers on your shoe, on your shoe
Put three fingers on your shoe, on your shoe
Put three fingers on your shoe, and leave it a day or two
Put three fingers on your shoe, on your shoe.

Repeat, changing objects to:
Put four fingers on your chin, . . . that's where the food slips in, *et cetera.*
Put five fingers on your cheek, . . . and leave them about a week, *et cetera.*
Put your fingers all together, . . . and we'll clap for better weather, *et cetera.*

1-2-3-4-5

Game: Place twelve numbers on the floor, ranging from one to five. Place children around numbers and have them march around numbers until a whistle is blown. When the whistle is blown, the children stop, pick up and identify number and count that number of children. The numbers are then replaced, and the game resumes.

Rhythmic Activities—Number Concepts

One Arm

Good game for the end of rest period.

One arm goes up, one arm goes down, one arm goes up and down.
Two arms go up, two arms go down, two arms go up and down.
One leg goes up, one leg goes down, one leg goes up and down.
Two legs go up, two legs go down, two legs go up and down.

Five Little Ducks

Five little ducks went in for a swim,
The first little duck put his head in.
The second little duck put his head back,
The third little duck said, "Quack, quack, quack."
The fourth little duck with his tiny brother
Went for a walk with his father and mother.

Five Little Kittens

Five little kittens
Sleeping on a chair,
One rolled off.
Four were still there.

Four little kittens,
One climbed a tree
To look in a bird's nest.
Then there were three.

Three little kittens
Playing in the sun,
One chased a ball.
Then there was one.

Two little kittens
Playing in the sun,
One chased a ball.
Then there was one.

One little kitten,
Fur as soft as silk,
Left all alone to
Drink a bowl of milk.

Johnny's Hammer

Johnny works with one hammer, one hammer, one hammer
This fine day.
Johnny works with two hammers, two hammers, two hammers
This fine day.

(Continue, merely change to "three," "four," and "five.")

Johnny now is so tired, so tired, so tired
This fine day.
Johnny goes to sleep now, sleep now, sleep now
This fine day.
Johnny wakes up now, up now, up now
This fine day.

Five Years Old

Please, everybody, look at me!
Today I'm five years old, you see!
And after this, I won't be four,
Not ever, ever, anymore!
I won't be three—or two—or one,
For that was when I'd first begun.
Now I'll be five a while, and then
I'll soon be something else again!

Five Little Squirrels

Five little squirrels
Up in a tree,
This little squirrel said,
"What do I see?"
This little squirrel said,
"I smell a gun."
This little squirrel said,

14

"Let's run."
This little squirrel said,
"Let's hide in the shade."
This little squirrel said,
"Hum, I'm not afraid."
When BANG went the gun,
And away they ran, every one.

Five Little Pigs

Five little piggies
Out to explore.
One got lost.
Then there were four.

Four little piggies,
How one did squeal
When three little piggies
Ate all his meal.

Three little piggies,
One likes to roam,
Two little piggies
Now left at home.

Two little piggies
Were eating a bun.
One fell in the trough.
Then there was one.

One little piggy
Squealing with delight
Found a red apple
And took a big bite.

Five Little Ants

Five little ants in an anthill,
Busily working and never still.
Do you think they are alive?
See them come out—
One, two, three, four, five.
These five little ants near an anthill
Run as hard and run with a will
To gather food to keep alive.
Now they go in—
One, two, three, four, five.

Ten Little Indians*

One little, two little, three little Indians,
Four little, five little, six little Indians,
Seven little, eight little, nine little Indians,
Ten little Indian boys [girls].

(Reverse order starting with ten little, down to one little Indian boy.)

(Raise one finger: keep raised as each finger is added consecutively. Lower one finger as the reverse order song is sung. Keep lowering until one is left.)

*From *Growth Through Play,* by A. M. Farina, S. H. Furth, and J. M. Smith (Englewood Cliffs: Prentice-Hall, 1959).

Happy Hands

Hands up high *(raise arms above head)*
Hands down low *(bend body and dangle arms)*
Hide those hands *(put hands behind back)*
Now where did they go? *(look around you)*
Out comes one *(bring one hand in front of your face)*
Now there's two *(bring out the other hand)*
Clap them *(close hands)*
Now we're through *(drop arms to sides)*

Counting Time

One—two
Cows that moo.
Two—three
Squirrels in a tree.
Three—four
Cats at the door.
Four—five
Bees in a hive.
Five—six
Little brown chicks.
Six—seven
Birds nearing heaven.
Seven—eight
Sheep at the gate.
Eight—nine
Ducks in a line.
Nine—ten
Pigs in a pen.

Counting Finger Play

With two hands and fingers, count to ten.
One to ten! Then back again!
Counting with fingers can be fun.
Let's play a game! We'll start with one!

*(Hold up two hands. Count with fingers.
One to ten, then ten to one.)*

Here is Susie! Here is Fred!
Next comes Sally! Then comes Ted!
Hello, Billy! Hello, Jim!
Come in, Betty! Come in, Tim!
Welcome, Mary! Welcome, Arty!
I'm so glad you all came to my birthday
    party!

*(Starting with thumb, raise each finger,
one by one, to count friends.)*

Come to the table! Each take a chair.
Look! A cake! Count the candles there!
One-two-three-four-five!
And one more to grow!
Huff and puff, and blow, blow, blow!

*(Hold up ten fingers. Bend, one by one.
Count with fingers.)*

*(Blow on candle fingers. Fold down, one
by one.)*

High-Heeled Shoes
by Kate Cox Goddard

I like to wear my mommie's shoes,
I mean the pair she doesn't use.
I pick the ones with highest heels,
You can't imagine how it feels.
To walk around, go out the door,
Clump, clumping all across the floor.

The Chickens

Said the first little chicken
With a queer little squirm,
"I wish I could find
A fat little worm."

Said the second little chicken
With an odd little shrug,
"I wish I could find
A fat little bug."

Said the third little chicken
With a sharp little squeal,
"I wish I could find
Some nice yellow meal."

Said the fourth little chicken
With a small sigh of grief,
"I wish I could find
A little green leaf."

Said the fifth little chicken
With a faint little moan,
"I wish I could find
A wee gravel stone."

"Now, see here," said the mother
From the green garden patch.
"If you want any breakfast,
Just come here and scratch."

Five Little Fishes

Five little fishes swimming in a pool.
First one said, "The pool is cool."
Second one said, "The pool is deep."
Third one said, "I want to sleep."
Fourth one said, "Let's take a dip."
Fifth one said, "I spy a ship."
Fisherman boat comes,
Line goes ker-splash,
Away the five little fishies dash.

Drinking Fountain
by Marchette Chute

When I climb up,
I get a drink.
It doesn't work
The way you think.

I turn it up.
The water goes
And hits me right
Upon the nose.

I turn it down
To make it small
And don't get any
Drink at all.

My Dog
by Marchette Chute

His nose is short and scrubby,
His ears hang rather low,
He always brings the stick back,
No matter how far you throw.

He gets spanked rather often
For things he shouldn't do,
Like lying on beds and barking,
And eating up shoes when they're new.

He always wants to be going
Where he isn't supposed to go.
He tracks up the house when it's snowing.
Oh! Puppy, I love you so.

Five Little Polar Bears

Five little polar bears
Playing on the shore.
One fell in the water,
And then there were four.

Four little polar bears
Swimming out to sea.
One got lost,
And then there were three.

Three little polar bears
Said, "What shall we do?"
One climbed an iceberg,
Then there were two.

Two little polar bears
Playing in the sun.
One went for food,
Then there was one.

One little polar bear
Didn't want to stay.
He said, "I'm lonesome,"
And swam far away.

Five Little Monkeys Jumping on the Bed

Five little monkeys jumping on the bed.
One fell off and cracked his head.
Mommy called the doctor, and the doctor said,
"No more monkeys jumping on the bed."
Four little monkeys jumping on the bed.
One fell off and cracked his head.
Mommy called the doctor, and the doctor said,
"No more monkeys jumping on the bed."

(Continue with three, two, and one.)

Last Verse:
One little monkey jumping on the bed.
He fell off and broke his head.
Mommy called the doctor, and the doctor said,
"No more monkeys jumping on the bed."
  Then there were no more monkeys jumping on the bed.

Fish Alive

One, two, three, four, five. I caught a fish alive.
Six, seven, eight, nine, ten. I let him go again.
Why did you let him go? Cause he bit my finger so.
Which one did he bite? The little one on the right.

Five Little Seashells

Five little seashells, lying on the shore;
Swish went the waves, and then there were four.
Four little seashells, cozy as could be;
Swish went the waves, and then there were three.
Three little seashells, all pearly and new,
Swish went the waves, and then there were two.
Two little seashells, sleeping in the sun,
Swish went the waves, and then there was one.
One little seashell, left all alone,
Whispered, "Shhhhhhh," as it took itself home.

Part II

Singing Activities: General Basis for a Music Curriculum for the Young Child

Introduction

Objectives

The children will gain in self-expression, memory, listening skills, participation, social studies, rhythm, enjoyment, relaxation, and satisfaction.

Benefits

- Practice in following directions
- Coordination of actions and words
- Social skills
- Development of balance and coordination
- Space awareness by following directions
- Practice in responding to visual cues
- Developing locomotor skills such as hopping, jumping, crawling, climbing, running, clapping, digging, and sliding
- Recognition of beat and sensing changes in tempo
- Establishment of concepts of tempo and dynamic range such as faster, slower, louder, and softer

The purpose of teaching music to the young child is to assist him to have a greater enjoyment of music. This enjoyment of music may be produced through listening, participating, or creating. Music appeals to the emotions and to the mind. The listener will gradually feel the rhythm of the music. When he begins to move his hands or feet to the rhythm, he is having a *new* experience, developing confidence, beginning coordination of the mind and the body, and releasing tension and energy.

Music for young children is much the same as for all children. They need and will appreciate the opportunity to experience and participate in music activities in all forms. In music for young children there is a constant shifting of emphasis. Goals are modified so that they are attainable in various handicapped conditions. The key issue in working with any child is to know his area of strength and build on it. Music should be a part of the child's total life pattern. In all curriculum areas one must learn as much about the nature of various problems as possible and then develop techniques and materials to meet the unique needs of the child. The young child has many learning styles. Some will show sensory modalities; some will show distractibility tendencies; some will show preservative tendencies; some will have problems in focusing and listening. Therefore, intimate knowledge of each child paves the way toward meeting individual needs.

The recent trend of placing special needs children with normal children in regular classrooms and in social groups should ensure that these children will receive the benefits of music in a natural setting. Music can offer the potential for growth that recognizes no handicap.

Needs of the young child are not unlike those of the other children, which are:

1. Security
2. Self-respect and self-gratification
3. Love and affection
4. Movement (whenever possible or depending on the handicap)
5. Positive interpersonal relationships
6. A sense of belonging, worth, and acceptance
7. A feeling of accomplishment and contribution

Songs and Rhythms

Every pre-school child or, indeed, all children have a right to lovely experiences with music. The fun and pleasure of singing, the joy of rhythm, and the intrigue of experimenting with musical instruments all have untold value for the young child.

Music experiences for pre-school children should be many and varied, and singing is one of the most satisfying experiences. Singing is definitely social and is pleasing to children particularly, because it is a happy experience. It is also a natural experience, for we find children making up little tunes and tiny songs or chants or merely humming while at play.

The pre-school child enjoys songs about children and their activities, animals, including birds, seasonal songs, and weather songs. Religious songs should be based largely upon familiar seasonal and native materials.

Selection Criteria

1. Words should be simple.
2. Repetition should be involved.
3. Songs should be based on child's interest.
4. Songs should be short, no more than one or two sentences.

For many years, pre-school children were limited to a diet of insipid music. It is only in recent years that we have learned, as our ancestors certainly must have known, that good folk music is fine fare for pre-school children. They like it funny; they like it silly; they like it dramatic. They even like it pathetic. Story songs like "The Cooper of Fife" or "Annie, the Miller's Daughter" can be shortened to one stanza. In all songs pre-school children should be encouraged to make up additional stanzas about the same topic or about themselves. Aside from singing and inventing new lyrics, activities at this age level involve pantomime, simple rhythmic play, or a combination of both. Here again you can encourage the children's native creative ability.

Music used in a planned program for the classroom and then as the need arises—to stimulate or to relax—may become an important factor in the social development of the children. They may attain satisfaction through self-expression and emotional release through listening or participating in music activities. Music may be taught for its own sake, as well as used in presenting subjects such as social studies, number readiness, and language arts. These should be integrated wherever possible.

24

The Activities

Hokey-Pokey

You put your right foot in, you put your right foot out,
You put your right foot in, and you shake it all about.
You do the Hokey-Pokey, and you turn yourself around.
That's what it's all about.

You put your left foot in, you put your left foot out,
You put your left foot in, and you shake it all about.
You do the Hokey-Pokey, and you turn yourself around.
That's what it's all about.

You put your right hand in, you put your right hand out,
You put your right hand in, and you shake it all about.
You do the Hokey-Pokey, and you turn yourself around.
That's what it's all about.

You put your left hand in, you put your left hand out,
You put your left hand in, and you shake it all about.
You do the Hokey-Pokey, and you turn yourself around.
That's what it's all about.

You put your head in, you put your head out,
You put your head in, and you shake it all about.
You do the Hokey-Pokey, and you turn yourself around.
That's what it's all about.

You put your backside in, you put your backside out,
You put your backside in, and you shake it all about.
You do the Hokey-Pokey, and you turn yourself around.
That's what it's all about.

You put your whole self in, you put your whole self out,
You put your whole self in, and you shake it all about.
You do the Hokey-Pokey, and you turn yourself around.
That's what it's all about.

Bow, Belinda

1. Bow, bow, bow, Belinda, bow, bow, bow, Belinda,
   Bow, bow, bow, Belinda, won't you be my partner?

2. Right hand out, oh, Belinda,
   Right hand out, oh, Belinda,
   Right hand out, oh, Belinda,
   Right hand out, and shake, shake, shake.

3. Left hand out, oh, Belinda,
   Left hand out, oh, Belinda,
   Left hand out, oh, Belinda,
   Left hand out and shake, shake, shake.

4. Both hands out, oh, Belinda,
   Both hands out, oh, Belinda,
   Both hands out, oh, Belinda,
   Both hands out, and shake, shake, shake.

5. Circle round, oh, Belinda,
   Circle round, oh, Belinda,
   Circle round, oh, Belinda,
   Won't you be my darling?

Children Needed: four to six ages 4–5.

Top

```
O                                              X
O                                              X
O                                              X
O                                              X
O                                              X
```

Bottom

Verse 1. Top O and Bottom X advance 3 steps toward the center, bow, take 4 steps back to his or her place (see above). Top X and Bottom O do the same.

Verse 2. Top O and Bottom X advance, join hands, turn in place, and retire. Top X and Bottom O do the same.

Verse 3. As above, but with left hands.

Verse 4. Continue through each verse.

Train Song

1. The train is a-coming, oh, yes!
   Train is a-coming, oh, yes!
   Train is a-coming,
   Train is a-coming, oh, yes!

26

2. Better get your ticket, oh, yes!
   Better get your ticket, oh, yes!
   Better get your ticket,
   Better get your ticket, oh, yes!

3. Room for many more, oh, yes!
4. Hear the whistle blow, oh, yes!
5. Hear the conductor calling, "All aboard!"
6. The train is a-leaving, oh, yes!
7. Now the wheels are rolling, oh, yes!
8. I'm on my way to Texas, oh, yes!

Hush Little Baby

1. Hush little baby, don't say a word,
       Mama's going to buy you a mockingbird.
2. If that mockingbird won't sing,
       Mama's going to buy you a diamond ring.
3. If that diamond ring turns brass,
       Mama's going to buy you a looking glass.
4. If that looking glass gets broke,
       Mama's going to buy you a billy goat.
5. If that billy goat gets bony,
       Mama's going to buy you a Shetland pony.
6. If that pony runs away,
       Mama's going to buy you another some day.

This Train

This train is bound for glory, this train,
This train is bound for glory, this train,
This train is bound for glory,
Don't ride no one but the good and holy,
This train is bound for glory, this train.

This bike is rolling downhill, this bike,
This bike is rolling downhill, this bike,
This bike is rolling downhill,
Over the bridge and by the old mill,
This bike is rolling downhill, this bike.

This plane is flying so fast, this plane,
This plane is flying so fast, this plane,
This plane is flying so fast,
Look real hard or it'll fly right past,
This plane is flying so fast, this plane.

This car belongs to daddy, this car,
This car belongs to daddy, this car,
This car belongs to daddy,
When it's dirty, daddy gets maddy,
This car belongs to daddy, this car.

This boat can sail to China, this boat,
This boat can sail to China, this boat,
This boat can sail to China,
Woo, woo, woo, says the ocean liner,
This boat can sail to China, this boat.

The Muffin Man

The first child sings:
    Do you know the Muffin Man,
    The Muffin Man, the Muffin Man?
    Do you know the Muffin Man,
    Who lives in Drury Lane?

The partner replies:
    Yes, I know the Muffin Man,
    The Muffin Man, the Muffin Man.
    Yes, I know the Muffin Man,
    Who lives in Drury Lane.

These two children continue to make the puppetlike movements together inside the circle, which stands, singing:

    Oh, to know the Muffin Man,
    The Muffin Man, the Muffin Man.
    Oh, to know the Muffin Man,
    Who lives in Drury Lane.

Tiny Tim

I had a little brother,
His name was Tiny Tim.
I put him in the bathtub
To see if he could swim.

He drank up all the water,
He ate up all the soap.
He died the next morning [or his tummy hurt that evening]
With a bubble in his throat.

In came the doctor,
In came the nurse,
In came the lady
With the alligator purse.

"Measles," said the doctor.
"Mumps," said the nurse.
"Chicken pox," said the lady
With the alligator purse.

"Penicillin," said the doctor.
"Penicillin," said the nurse.
"Penicillin," said the lady
With the alligator purse.

I don't want the doctor!
I don't want the nurse!
I don't want the lady
With the alligator purse.

Out walked the doctor,
Out walked the nurse,
Out walked the lady
With the alligator purse.

Peter Hammers

Peter hammers with one hammer, one hammer, one hammer;
Peter hammers with one hammer all day long.

Peter hammers with two hammers, two hammers, two hammers;
Peter hammers with two hammers all day long.

Peter hammers with three hammers, three hammers, three hammers;
Peter hammers with three hammers all day long.

Peter hammers with four hammers, four hammers, four hammers;
Peter hammers with four hammers all day long.

Peter hammers with five hammers, five hammers, five hammers;
Peter hammers with five hammers all day long.

(very slow)
Peter's very tired now, tired now, tired now;
Peter's very tired now all day long.

(fast)
Peter's wide awake now, awake now, awake now;
Peter's wide awake now all day long.

29

He's Got the Whole World in His Hands

He's got the whole world in His hands,
He's got the whole world in His hands,
He's got the whole world in His hands,
He's got the whole world in His hands.

He's got the little bitty baby in His hands,
He's got the little bitty baby in His hands,
He's got the little bitty baby in His hands,
He's got the whole world in His hands.

He's got you and me, brother, in His hands,
He's got you and me, brother, in His hands,
He's got you and me, brother, in His hands,
He's got the whole world in His hands.

Pop Goes the Weasel

All around the cobbler's bench,
The monkey chased the weasel.
The monkey thought 'twas all in fun,
Pop goes the weasel.

A penny for a spool of thread,
A penny for a needle.
That's the way the money goes,
Pop goes the weasel.

Bluebird, Bluebird

1. Bluebird, bluebird, through my window
Bluebird, bluebird, through my window
Bluebird, bluebird, through my window
Bluebird, bluebird, aren't you tired?
2. Take a little child and tap 'em on the shoulder
Take a little child and tap 'em on the shoulder
Take a little child and tap 'em on the shoulder
Bluebird, bluebird, aren't you tired?

Old MacDonald Had a Band

(Ages 3–8)

1. Old MacDonald had a band—E-I-E-I-Oh.
   And in his band, he had some feet—E-I-E-I-Oh.
   With a stamp, stamp here; stamp, stamp there
   Here's a stamp, there's a stamp,
   Everywhere a stamp, stamp.
   Old MacDonald had a band—E-I-E-I-Oh.
2. And in his band he had some hands—E-I-E-I-Oh.
   With a clap, clap, here, *et cetera.*
3. And in his band he had some knees—E-I-E-I-Oh.
   With a bend, bend here, *et cetera.*
4. And in his band he had some heads—E-I-E-I-Oh.
   With a bow, bow here, *et cetera.*

Jack-in-the-box

Jack-in-the-box is out of sight,
When the cover's fasten'd tight;
Touch the spring, and up he goes,
Jack-in-the-box with his long red nose.

Jack-in-the-box, still as a mouse,
Deep down inside his little dark house;
Jack-in-the-box, resting so still,
Will you come out? Yes, I will!

This Old Man

This old man, he played one,
He played knick-knack on my thumb,
With a knick-knack, paddy wack,
Give the dog a bone.
This old man came rolling home.

This old man, he played two,
He played knick-knack on my shoe,
With a knick-knack, paddy wack,
Give the dog a bone,
This old man came rolling home.

This old man, he played three,
He played knick-knack on my knee,
With a knick-knack, paddy wack,
Give the dog a bone,
This old man came rolling home.

This old man, he played four,
He played knick-knack on my door,
With a knick-knack, paddy wack,
Give the dog a bone,
This old man came rolling home.

This old man, he played five,
He played knick-knack on my hive,
With a knick-knack, paddy wack,
Give the dog a bone,
This old man came rolling home.

This old man, he played six,
He played knick-knack on my sticks,
With a knick-knack, paddy wack,
Give the dog a bone,
This old man came rolling home.

On Top of Spaghetti

1. On top of spaghetti
   All covered with cheese,
   I lost my poor meatball
   When somebody sneezed.
2. It rolled off the table
   And onto the floor,
   And then my poor meatball
   Rolled out the door.
3. It rolled in the garden
   And under a bush,
   And then my poor meatball
   Was nothing but mush.
4. The mush was as tasty
   As tasty could be,
   And early next summer
   It grew into a tree.
5. The tree was all covered
   With beautiful moss,
   It grew lovely meatballs
   And tomato sauce.
6. So if you eat spaghetti
   All covered with cheese,
   Hold onto your meatballs
   And don't ever sneeze.

Shoo Fly

Shoo fly, don't bother me,
Shoo fly, don't bother me,
Shoo fly, don't bother me,
For I belong to somebody.
I feel, I feel, I feel,
I feel like a morning star,
I feel, I feel, I feel,
I feel like a morning star.

Old Joe Clark

Round around old Joe Clark,
Round around I say,
Round around old Joe Clark,
I ain't got long to stay.

Old Joe Clark he had a house,
Sixteen stories high.
Every story in that house
Was full of chicken pie.

Old Joe Clark he had a dog,
As blind as he could be.
Chased a redbug 'round the stump
And a coon up a hollow tree.

I went down to Old Joe's house,
Never been there before.
He slept on the feather bed,
And I slept on the floor.

Old Joe Clark he had a cat,
Smart as he could be.
Taught him how to add and subtract
And to multiply by three.

Old Joe Clark he had a wife,
As blind as she could be.
She chased him around the backyard pump
And then up a hickory tree.

33

Jenny Crack Corn

Jenny crack corn and I don't care.
Jenny crack corn and I don't care.
Jenny crack corn and I don't care.
Today's a holiday.

Round and round and I don't care.
Round and round and I don't care.
Round and round and I don't care.
Now let's all stand still.

Right hand up and I don't care.
Right hand up and I don't care.
Right hand up and I don't care.
Turn the other way.

Left hand up and I don't care.
Left hand up and I don't care.
Left hand up and I don't care.
Turn right back again.

Both hands up and I don't care.
Both hands up and I don't care.
Both hands up and I don't care.
Circle round again.

Jenny crack corn and I don't care.
Jenny crack corn and I don't care.
Jenny crack corn and I don't care.
Today's a holiday.

She'll Be Comin' 'round the Mountain

She'll be comin' 'round the mountain when she comes. Toot, toot!
She'll be comin' 'round the mountain when she comes. Toot, toot!
She'll be comin' 'round the mountain, she'll be comin' round the mountain,
She'll be comin' 'round the mountain when she comes. Toot, toot!

She'll be riding six white horses when she comes. Whoa, whoa!
She'll be riding six white horses when she comes. Whoa, whoa!
She'll be riding six white horses, she'll be riding six white horses,
She'll be riding six white horses when she comes. Whoa, whoa! Toot, toot!

And we'll all go out to meet her when she comes. "Hi there!"
And we'll all go out to meet her when she comes. "Hi there!"
And we'll all go out to meet her, and we'll all go out to meet her,
And we'll all go out to meet her when she comes. "Hi there!" Whoa, whoa! Toot toot!

Then we'll kill that old red rooster when she comes. Chop, chop!
Then we'll kill that old red rooster when she comes. Chop, chop!
Then we'll kill that old red rooster, then we'll kill that old red rooster,
Then we'll kill that old red rooster when she comes. Chop, chop! "Hi there!" Whoa, whoa!
    Toot, toot!

And we'll all have chicken and dumplings when she comes. Yum, yum!
And we'll all have chicken and dumplings when she comes. Yum, yum!
And we'll all have chicken and dumplings, and we'll all have chicken and dumplings,
And we'll all have chicken and dumplings when she comes. Yum, yum! Chop, chop! "Hi
    there!" Whoa, whoa! Toot, toot!

A Peanut Was Sitting on a Railroad Track

A peanut was sitting on a railroad track,
Her heart was all a-flutter.
The 8:15 came roaring past,
Toot! Toot! Peanut butter!

The Little White Duck

There's a little white duck sitting in the water,
A little white duck doing what he oughter,
He took a bite of a lily pad,
Flapped his wings, and he said, "I'm glad
I'm a little white duck sitting in the water. Quack, quack, quack."

There's a little green frog swimming in the water,
A little green frog doing what he oughter,
He jumped right off of the lily pad
That the little duck bit, and he said, "I'm glad
I'm a little green frog swimming in the water. Glumph, glumph, glumph."

There's a little black bug floating on the water,
A little black bug doing what he oughter,
He tickled the frog on the lily pad
That the little duck bit, and he said, "I'm glad
I'm a little black bug floating on the water. Chirp, chirp, chirp."

There's a little red snake lying in the water,
A little red snake doing what he oughter,
He frightened the duck and the frog so bad,
He ate the little bug, and he said, "I'm glad
I'm a little red snake lying in the water. Sss, Sss, Sss."

Now there's nobody left sitting in the water,
Nobody left doing what he oughter,
There's nothing left but the lily pad,
The duck and the frog ran away. It's sad
That there's nobody left sitting in the water. Boo, boo, boo.

Jim along Josie

Hey Jim along, Jim along Josie.
Hey Jim along, Jim along Joe.

Hop, hop along, Jim along Josie.
Hop, hop along, Jim along Joe.

Run, run along, Jim along Josie.
Run, run along, Jim along Joe.

Crawl, crawl along, Jim along Josie.
Crawl, crawl along, Jim along Joe.

Walk, walk along, Jim along Josie.
Walk, walk along, Jim along Joe.

Jump, roll, skip, tiptoe, *et cetera*.

Where Is Thumbkin?

Where is thumbkin? Where is thumbkin?
Here I am, here I am.
How are you today, sir?
Very well, I thank you.
Run away, run away.

Where is pointer? Where is pointer?
Here I am, here I am.
How are you today, sir?
Very well, I thank you.
Run away, run away.

Where is middle? Where is middle?
Here I am, here I am.
How are you today, sir?
Very well, I thank you.
Run away, run away.

Where is ringer? Where is ringer?
Here I am, here I am.
How are you today, sir?
Very well, I thank you.
Run away, run away.

Where is pinky? Where is pinky?
Here I am, here I am.
How are you today, sir?
Very well, I thank you.
Run away, run away.

Part III
Poetry

Introduction

Objectives

The children will succeed in poise, speech and language, memory, and dramatization.

Benefits

- Auditory skills
- Opportunity for imaginative play
- Development of speech and language
- Auditory memory (the child must remember what comes first, anticipate what's next, et cetera)
- Matching of actions to words, gives practice in acting out position words such as *up, down, out,* and *in*
- Body awareness
- Building attention and concentration
- Development of auditory discrimination, as in comparing the sounds of two words for rhyming qualities
- Vocabulary development, identification of body parts
- Coordination of action and words

> A teacher who can arouse a feeling for one single good poem accomplishes more than he who fills our memory with rows on rows of natural objects, classified with names and form.
>
> —Johann W. Von Goethe

Poetry is pure cadenced delight transmitted spontaneously from the teacher to the pupil. It is stored in the mind and quoted whenever it seems appropriate. Children love the rhythm and the rhyme and learn new words correctly and painlessly. Poetry is so flexible that it fits in anywhere beautifully, appropriately, and, years later, nostalgically. But so much of it depends on the teacher. Poetry is important.

The teacher who makes time in every busy day to read or recite a poem gives her pupils a rich heritage. Poetry helps us recapture a memory of an experience which we can easily recall when needed.

A navy chaplain explained it this way: "Before battle, I had a book from which I was to quote to give courage and solace to the men. I never used it. Each man would recall a fragment of poetry and comfort himself saying, 'Well, as my mother used to say,————.' "

Poetry "is the safe-kept memory of a lovely thing," as Sara Teasdale once remarked. Every teacher has the opportunity to build these poetic memories.

The teacher who teaches young children three to eight years old will find poetry a stabilizing influence in her classroom. When a small child falls down and is apt to cry, a quick response with a few lines of poetry quoted by the teacher removes all signs of excitement. Try a short rhyme such as:

Hurrah, for Bobby Bumble
He never minds a tumble
But up he jumps
And rubs his bumps
Hurrah, for Bobby Bumble.

Soon the children will join in the comforting rhyme, sometimes substituting the name of the injured one for Bobby.

At other times when children are emotionally disturbed, the suggested "Let's say The Swing poem, and then we'll sing the second part" eliminates uneasiness.

Poetry belongs in the daily schedule not just for therapeutic reasons but for fun and enrichment. The techniques for helping children enjoy and learn poems are very simple. The teacher must read or recite well aloud, must be acquainted with many sources of poetry, and should be able to recite a variety of poems. Small children watch the teacher's expression as she enjoys saying the poems to them. A teacher may notice favorite activity in her class. All the children are making buildings or houses. The poem "Buildings" would add zest to their day:

Buildings

Buildings are a great surprise
Every one's a different size
Offices
  grow
    long
      and
        high,
          tall
            enough
              to
                touch
                  the
                    sky.

Houses seem
more like a box,
made of blue
and building blocks.

Every time you look you see
Buildings shaped quite differently.

In the classroom, as every teacher knows, it's different. Each of the poems in this guide was selected with this difference in mind. They were also chosen expressly for a teacher to

42

read and act out aloud with her class. Every selection invites the listeners' participation—vocal, physical, or emotional.

The selections cover an extensive range of activities for the young child including their interests and experiences. Many of the poems in this guide offer a few suggestions for reading readiness, participation, or possible discussion. A poem can simply be enjoyed for its own sake.

In reading a poem, there should be enthusiasm, excitement, and joy. It is the author's hope that the poems in this guide will help you transmit to your boys and girls the joy of poetry.

A few hints on reading poetry to children: If you enjoy reading poetry yourself, just remember to:

1. Read the poem aloud to yourself before you try it on your class.
2. Read slowly enough so that children can absorb the images or the ideas.
3. Read naturally, expressing whatever feelings you really feel. Do not adopt a special hushed, poetry-reading voice.

Remember—if you're enthusiastic, your children will be, too.

The Poems

The Squirrel

Whisky, frisky,
Hippity hop,
Up he goes
To the treetop!

Whirly, twirly,
Round and round,
Down he scampers
To the ground.

Furly, curly,
What a tail!
Tall as a feather,
Broad as a sail!

Where's his supper?
In the shell.
Snappity, crackity,
Out it fell!

Who Lives Here?

Who lives in a nest
High up in a tree?
Who lives in a hole
In a home you can't see?

Who lives in a house
With a roof and a door
With windows to look out
And a ceiling and floor?

A rabbit lives in a hole.
A bird lives in a nest.
I live in a house,
And I like my home best!

Snow
by Dorothy Aldis

The fence posts wear marshmallow hats
On a snowy day,
Bushes in their night gowns
Are kneeling down to pray,
And all the trees have silver skirts
And want to dance away.

The Rabbit Skip
by Margaret Wise Brown

Hop Skip Jump
A rabbit won't bite.

Hop Skip Jump
A rabbit won't fight.

Hop Skip Jump
A rabbit runs light.

Hop Skip Jump
He's out of sight.

The Woodpecker*
by Elizabeth Modox Roberts

The woodpecker pecked out a little round hole,
And made him a house in the telephone pole.

One day when I watched, he poked out his head,
And he had on a hood and a collar of red.

When the streams of rain pour out of the sky,
And the sparkles of lightning go flashing by,

And the big, big wheels of thunder roll,
He can snuggle back in the telephone pole.

*Copyright 1922 by B. W. Huebsch, Inc., 1950 by Ivor S. Roberts. Reprinted by permission of Viking Press, Inc., New York.

The Merry-Go-Round

I climbed up on the merry-go-round,
And it went round and round.

I climbed up on the big horse brown,
And it went up and down.

Around and round
And up and down,
Around and round
And up and down.

I sat high up on a big brown horse
And rode around.

On the merry-go-round
And rode around.

On the merry-go-round
Around
And round
And
Round.

On Our Way
by Eve Merriam

What kind of walk shall we take today?
Leap like a frog? Creep like a snail?
Scamper like a squirrel with a furry tail?

Flutter like a butterfly? Chicken peck?
Stretch like a turtle with a poking out neck?

Trot like a pony, clip clop clop?
Swing like a monkey in a tree top?

Scuttle like a crab? Kangaroo jump?
Plod like a camel with an up-and-down hump?

We could even try a brand new way—
Walking down the street
On our own two feet.

Valentine Surprise

I have something behind my back—   *Hide hands behind back.*
Something just for you!

Is it something in a box?   *Shake head no.*
Is it green or blue?   *Shake head no.*

Is it red and pretty?   *Nod head yes twice.*
Is it really mine?   *Nod head yes.*

Here it is with lots of love—   *Bring hands to front. Index fingers touch,*
A great big Valentine!   *move apart, up, to right, and down to*
          a point to make a heart shape.

The Balloon Man

Our balloon man has balloons.
He holds them on a string.
He blows his horn and walks about
Through puddles, in the spring.

He stands on corners while they bob
And tug above his head.
Green balloons and blue balloons
And yellow ones and red.

He takes our pennies and unties
The two we choose, and then
He turns around and waves his hand
And blows his horn again.

February Second

Two may perform this action play. One is a groundhog. One is a shadow.

Down in his burrow, deep below the ground,   *Groundhog curls into ball with head*
          down, asleep. wakes, stretches,
          yawns.

Groundhog wakes up and begins to stir
     around.
"I've slept enough! On this February day,
I think it would be nice to go up and play!"

48

Up up up! He pokes his head out, *Gets up slowly, head stretches up, looks*
Looks this way and that way—looks all about. *all around.*
Then out jumps Groundhog. The day is clear *Jumps.*
    and bright.
He sits beside his hole in the warm sunlight *Sits down.*
Sneaking up behind him, Groundhog does not *Shadow creeps up behind Groundhog.*
    see,
Shadow comes a-creeping, quiet as can be
Groundhog looks around. He trembles with *Groundhog looks over shoulder—trembles.*
    great fear!
"Boo!" shouts Shadow. "Get out of here! *Groundhog dives down—*
    curls up in ball again.

Shoo! Shoo, Groundhog! You cannot stay!" *Shadow makes shooing and waving*
    motions.

Down scurries Groundhog until another day!

The Turtle

There once was a turtle,
He lived in a box,
He swam in a puddle,
He climbed on the rocks,
He snapped at a mosquito,
He snapped at a flea,
He snapped at a minnow,
He snapped at me,
He caught the mosquito,
He caught the flea,
He caught the minnow,
But he didn't catch me.

The Elephant

Here comes the elephant
Swaying along
With his cargo of children
All singing a song.
To the tinkle of laughter
He goes on his way,
And his cargo of children
Have crowned him with May.
His legs are in leather
And padded his toes,
He can root up an oak
With a whisk of his nose.

49

With the wave of his trunk
And a turn of his chin
He can pull down a house
Or pick up a pin.
Beneath his gray forehead
A little eye peers.
Of what is he thinking
Between those wide ears?
If he wished to tease,
He could twirl his keeper
Over the trees.
If he were not kind
With Robert and Helen and Uncle Paul.
But that gray forehead,
Those crinkled ears,
Have learned to be kind in a hundred years.
And so with the children
He goes on his way
To the tinkle of laughter
And crowned with the May.

Turkey Gobbler
by Dorothy Stillman

A peacock can open his tail like a fan.
A parrot can speak so you think he's a man.
A pigeon can roost on the edge of a pan.
But only a turkey can gobble.

A peacock can strut like a king with a crown.
A parrot can swing with his head hanging down.
A pigeon can puff out his chest like a clown.
But only a turkey can gobble.

If I were a peacock, I wouldn't be proud.
If I were a parrot, I wouldn't talk loud.
A pigeon is nice, but if I were allowed,
I'd just be a turkey and gobble!

Teddy Bear

1. Teddy Bear, Teddy Bear, turn around
   Teddy Bear, Teddy Bear, touch the ground
   Teddy Bear, Teddy Bear, reach up high
   Teddy Bear, Teddy Bear, touch the sky
   Teddy Bear, Teddy Bear, close the door
   Teddy Bear, Teddy Bear, touch the floor.

2. Teddy Bear, Teddy Bear, touch your nose
   Teddy Bear, Teddy Bear, touch your toes
   Teddy Bear, Teddy Bear, show me how you eat
   Teddy Bear, Teddy Bear, touch your feet
   Teddy Bear, Teddy Bear, show me upstairs
   Teddy Bear, Teddy Bear, say your prayers.

Plunk, Plunk, Plunk

Flap, flap, flap, go the elephant's ears,
And his feet go plunk, plunk, plunk;
Monstrous he looks as he lumbers along,
Waving his great big trunk.
He is the smartest and bravest of all,
He looks almost as big as a house;
But it's the funniest thing that I know—
He's afraid of a wee little mouse.

The First Thanksgiving
by Elsie Lindgren

The woods were deep, the rocky ground
Was hard to farm, the Pilgrims found,
The Indians here were kind
To show the secret place where
Deer and turkeys could be snared.
Then red and pale face in the fall
Have a great feast, one and all.
"Now as the harvest season ends,
Let us meet," they said, "as friends
And give our thanks to God, who made
All men brothers, unafraid."

The Camel's Hump

The camel's hump is an ugly lump
Which well you may see at the zoo,
But uglier yet is the hump we get
From having too little to do.

Kiddies and grown-ups too-oo-oo,
If we haven't enough to do-oo-oo,
We get the hump—
Cameleelious hump—
The hump that is black and blue.

We climb out of bed with a frouzly head
And a snarly-yarly voice,
We shiver and scowl and we grunt and we growl
At our bath and our books and our toys.

And there ought to be a corner for me
(And I know there is one for you)
When we get the hump—
Cameleelious hump—
The hump that is black and blue.

The cure for this ill is not to sit still
Or frowst with a book by the fire,
But to take a large hoe and shovel also
And dig till you gently perspire.

Holding Hands

Elephants walking along the trails
Are holding hands by holding tails;
Trunks and tails are handy things
When elephants walk in circus rings;
Elephants work and elephants play,
And elephants walk and feel so gay;
And when they walk, it never fails,
They're holding hands by holding tails.

Popcorn
by Nancy Byrd Turner

Say a verse of popcorn
When a snow storm rage;
Fifty little brown men
Put into a cage;
Shake them till they laugh and leap
Crowding to the top;
Watch them burst their little coats
POP!!   POP!!   POP!!

Mr. and Mrs. Santa Claus

"Are the reindeer in the rain, dear?"
Asked Mrs. Santa Claus.
"No, I put them in the barn, dear,
To dry their little paws."

"Is the sleigh, sir, put away, sir,
In the barn beside the deer?"
"Yes, I'm going to get it ready
To use again next year."

"And the pack, dear, is it packed, dear?"
"Yes, it's empty of its toys,
And tomorrow I'll start filling it
For next year's girls and boys."

When You Talk to a Monkey
by Rowen Bennett

When you talk to a monkey
He seems very wise.
He scratches his head
And he blinks both his eyes;
But he won't say a word.
He just swings on a rail
And makes a big question mark
Out of his tail.

Who Lived in a Shoe?
by Beatrix Potter

You know that old woman
Who lived in a shoe?
She had so many children
She didn't know what to do?

I think if she lived in
A little shoe-house
That little old lady was
Surely a mouse!

First of All You Trace a Nickel

First of all you trace a nickel.
Then you add a little pickle.
Add three more for company.
Can you tell what this will be?

At the side you make a thing
Which turns out to be a wing.

At the bottom make a twig,
Then another just as big.

Head and neck these lines will be.
Now you do an eye to see.
More can easily be made.
Watch the turkeys on parade.

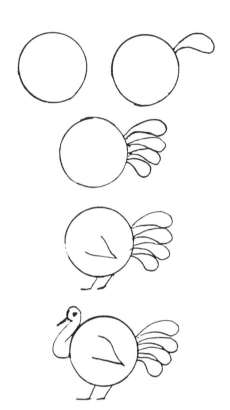

54

Lollipop Licks

One lick, two licks, three licks, four,
Skipping home from the candy store.
Five licks, six licks, seven licks, eight,
Open the latch on the garden gate.

Nine licks, ten licks, knock at the door.
Five licks and five licks make ten licks more.
Here is Mother! Take one big lick!
Look! There's nothing left but a lollipop stick!

One hand, fingers together, touch top of thumb to make big circle. Fingertips move down on thumb—circle gets a tiny bit smaller each time. Do this four times. Skip. Do four times more. Other hand makes opening motion. Do two more times. Other hand knocks. Do five more times. Circle very tiny, tongue takes big lick. Circle closes. First finger pops straight up.

Good Morning
by Muriel Sipe

One day I saw a downy duck,
With feathers on his back;
I said, "Good morning, downy duck,"
And he said, "Quack, Quack, Quack."

One day I saw a timid mouse,
He was so shy and meek;
I said, "Good morning, timid mouse,"
And he said, "Squeak, Squeak, Squeak."

One day I saw a curly dog,
I met him with a bow;
I said, "Good morning, curly dog,"
And he said, "Bow-Wow-Wow."

One day I saw a scarlet bird,
He woke me from my sleep;
I said, "Good morning, scarlet bird,"
And he said, "Cheep, Cheep, Cheep."

The Circus Parade

Oh, goody, it's coming, the circus parade,
And all the way up the street
What crowds of people in gay-colored clothes,
With popcorn and peanuts to eat.

The children have red, blue, and yellow balloons
As up by the curbing they stand,
And now, in the distance, we suddenly hear
The circus's big brass band.

Behind the crash-bang of the music they play
Come riders in red velvet gowns
And after them doing the funniest things
A silly procession of clowns.

Then lions and tigers that pace up and down
In wagons all painted with gold
And monkeys a-playing just all kinds of tricks,
As they grimace and chatter and scold.

Oh, next there come camels and elephants, too;
High on their back men ride;
There are queer little ponies, no bigger than dogs,
With a clown on a donkey beside.

And then there come chariots rumbling by
With horses all four in a row
And the wheezing old piping calliope at
The very tail end of the show.

Clouds
by Christina Rossetti

White sheep, white sheep
On a blue hill,
When the wind stops,
You all stand still,
When the wind blows,
You walk away slow
White sheep, white sheep,
Where do you go?

The Circus

The brass band blares,
The naptha flares,
The sawdust smells,
Showmen ring bells,
And oh, right into the circus ring
Comes such a lovely, lovely thing.
A milk-white pony with flying tress
And a beautiful lady,
A *beautiful* lady in a pink dress.
The red-and-white clown
For joy tumbles down,
Like a pink rose,
Round she goes,
On her tiptoes,
With the pony under,
And then, oh, wonder.
The pony, his milk-white tresses droop,
And the beautiful lady,
The *beautiful* lady,
Flies like a bird through the paper hoop.
The red-and-white clown for joy falls dead.
Then he waggles his feet and stands on his head,
And the little boys on the two-penny seats
Scream with laughter and suck their sweets.

Tails
by Rowena Bennett

The kangaroo has a heavy tail,
She sits on it for a chair.
There's scarcely any tail at all
Upon the polar bear.
But the monkey has the nicest tail
Of any living thing,
For he can hook it to a branch
And use it as a swing.

Part IV
Choral Speaking

Introduction

Objectives

The children will be successful in speech and language, social aspects, oral language, body awareness, imagination, self-help skills, and individuality.

Benefits

- Development of concentration skills
- Memory skills and attending to the task involved
- Feeling of security and unity
- Group solidarity, humor, and togetherness
- Social skills
- Encouragement of trust and togetherness in groups
- Stimulation of interest in other children
- Group concentration
- Social give and take
- Development of visual and auditory memory

Choral speaking results when a group of speakers is trained to recite poetry under leadership. Some students get satisfaction from expressing themselves but are too timid to speak alone. They lose self-consciousness in the group. If conducted properly, choral speaking is valuable in the classroom from both speech and social aspects.

Choral speaking may have many individual and combined objectives. Stopping at various places teaches the child how to breathe properly. Some poems, such as "Open, Shut Them" (p. 76), teach body awareness, so necessary to some exceptional children. Others, such as "Snoopy's Walk in the Rain," can teach self-help skills. Still others may have a math objective, as in "Five Little Chickadees" (p. 71). All activities may vary according to the ability and exceptionality of the child.

There sometimes will be a tendency toward sameness. The teacher must guard against this. She must help students visualize word pictures and get clear images.

The use and objectives of choral speaking are limited only by the imagination of the instructor.

Choral speaking has multiple virtues. It is a cooperative activity but permits brief solo work at times. It uses new words in correct content, thus teaching vocabulary. It stresses correct enunciation and a due regard for the amenities of punctuation, both in pacing and in inflection. Above all, it familiarizes the child with the beauty of words and thought.

Psychologically, it makes the *aggressive child* a part of the group and permits the *shy child* to feel of equal worth. The child who feels inadequate is no longer conspicuous; he has his own version of the poem, and he is able to follow and join with the others on an equal basis. Choral speaking can be a source of great pleasure. There are many values accruing from choral speaking:

1. It may be just the pinprick a class needs to involve it in an activity in which all may participate.
2. Planning how they will say the poem is of great psychological value to the children. They feel a sense of responsibility.
3. While interpreting a choral speaking selection, they learn to appreciate humorous situations and everyday happenings.
4. Striving to improve their verse choir, they improve their clarity of speech and oral readings.
5. Including choral speaking selections relating to *number readiness* enriches this particular area of the curriculum.
6. Participating with a group choir is of inestimable value to pupils from any culture.
7. The sharing of the final production with one's peers is the greatest reward for the children in a choral speaking group.

The Activities

Who Stole the Cookie from the Cookie Jar?

Have the children sit in a circle and begin a simple clapping pattern, and all children clap and chant together.

Group: Who stole the cookie from the cookie jar?
Teacher: [Name a child] stole the cookie from the cookie jar.
Child: Who, me?
Group: Yes, you!
Child: Couldn't be.
Group: Then who? Oh, yes! Oh, yes! Oh, yes!

Group: Who stole the cookie from the cookie jar? *Now the clapping begins with the child who was "it" picking the next child who is accused.*

"It": [Name another child] stole the cookie from the cookie jar.

This format should continue until all the children have been named as the thief. It might be helpful for the teacher to chant all lines with the children until they have a solid feeling for the question and answer concept. At first there will be interruptions and pauses in the game, but this goal should be kept in mind: the rhyme should be chanted with clapping and passed from child to child without interruptions, as perpetual motion, until each child has had a turn.

My Aunt Came Back

My aunt came back from old Algiers,
And she brought me back a pair of shears.

My aunt came back from Holland too,
And she brought me back a wooden shoe.

My aunt came back from old Japan,
And she brought me back a paper fan.

My aunt came back from old Belgium,
And she brought me back some bubble gum.

63

My aunt came back from the county fair,
And she brought me back a rocking chair.

My aunt came back from old Chile,
And she brought me back an itchy flea.

My aunt came back from the city zoo,
And she brought me back a nut like you!

Aunt Dinah's Gone

Leader: Aunt Dinah's gone!
Class (echoes): Aunt Dinah's gone!

Leader: Aunt Dinah's gone!
Class: Aunt Dinah's gone.

Leader: Well, how did she leave?
Class: Well, how did she leave?

Leader: Oh, how did she leave?
Class: Oh, how did she leave?

Leader: Well, she left like this. *(Leader assumes another pose.)*
Class (imitates): Oh, she left like this.

Leader: Oh, she left like this. *(Leader assumes any pose.)*
Class (imitates): Oh, she left like this.

All: She lives in the country,
Gonna move to town,
Gonna shake and shimmy *(everybody shake and shimmy)*
Till the sun goes down.

The Little Red Box

1. If I had my little red box
To put my good girls [boys] in,
I'd take them out and *(make kiss-kiss-kiss sounds)*
And put them back again.

2. If I had a little red box,
To put my bad girls [boys] in,
I'd take them out and *(clap-clap-clap)*
And put them back again.

3. If we had a big red box
   To put our good friends in,
   We'd take them out and *(everybody hug)*
   And put them back again.

Spring
by Lela K. Waltrip

Spring is in the swamp land.
   How do I know?
I can see from my tree-house
   The signs down below.

Wild flags and pink hyacinths
   Bloom along the way.
Insects peeping out of holes
   Are singing songs today.

Big green frogs are croaking
   From every lily pad.
'Tis the most glorious feeling
   A boy ever had.

Snowmen Fade Away
(Good for Illustration)

Six little snowmen
Standing in a row,
Each with a hat
And a big red bow.

Six little snowmen
Dressed for a show,
Now they are ready,
Where will they go?

Wait 'til the sun shines,
Soon they will go,
Down through the fields
With the melting snow.

My Shadow
by Ethel Hawthorne Tewksbury

A shadow is a funny thing,
For it can dance and flutter,
But not a single little word
Can any shadow utter!

I wonder if it sometimes would
Just like a chance to sputter,
Instead of trailing me about
With not a line to stutter!

The Man and the Goat

1. There was a man,
   Now please take note,
   There was a man
   Who had a goat.
2. He loved that goat,
   Indeed he did,
   He loved that goat
   Just like a kid.
3. One day that goat
   Felt frisk and fine,
   Ate three red shirts
   From off the clothesline.
4. Man grabbed that goat
   Right by his back
   And tied him to
   The railroad track.
5. And as the train
   Pulled into sight
   That goat grew pale
   And green with fright.
6. He heaved a sign
   As if in pain,
   Coughed up those shirts,
   And flagged down the train.

My Teddy Bear

My teddy bear's the greatest pet.
His ribbon's shiny red.
He never smells like Tommy's dog
He sleeps with me in bed.

He snuggles here beside me
On the pillow Mommy fluffed,
And I never have to feed him
'Cause he's already stuffed.

(After learning the words to the poem, children will recite by choral speaking, thus increasing speech and language skills)

Hands

Sometimes my hands are naughty;
And so my mother said
That she would have to spank them
And send them off to bed.
So little hands, be careful please
Of everything you do,
Because if you are sent to bed
I have to go there to.

On Halloween

Girls: When the haunted house is dark,
Boys: When the ghosties have a lark!
All: WHOO! WHOO! WHOO!
Girls: When the witches sweep the sky,
Boys: Then the hooty owls cry,
All: WHO? WHO? WHO?

Girls: When the gray mist huddles down,
Boys: Then the goblins race through town!
All: OOH! OOH! OOH!
Girls: We make believe, this scary night,
Boys: In Jack-o-lantern's cheery light!
All: Boo! Boo! Boo!

Tommy's Pumpkin

It was the biggest pumpkin that you have ever seen,
It grew in Tommy's garden on the night of Halloween.

He took a knife and cut the top, then scooped it with a spoon,
Made two round eyes, almost like this, and a mouth just like a moon.

He put a candle in it, and as quietly as a mouse,
He crept up and put it in the window of his house.

And Tommy's mother cried, "Oh, dear!
I fear, somebody must be hiding very near!"

Thanksgiving Dinner

Every day when we eat our dinner,
Our table is so small,
Just room for Mother, Father,
Sister, Baby, and me, that's all,
But when Thanksgiving comes, and company,
You can't believe your eyes,
That very same old table
Stretches out until this size!

My Funny Umbrella

All: Oh, isn't it fun when the rain comes down?
Solo 1: I like to go walking way down in the town.
Boys: The wind blows in gusts with all of its might
Girls: And makes my umbrella dance just like a kite.
Solo 2: I wave first to one side,
Solo 3: And then back it flies.
Solo 4: To sail off without me it certainly tries!
Solo 5: One day I had walked and was home—just about—
All: And my funny umbrella turned right inside out.

Halloween

All: Look outside! What a sight!
     All the spooks are out tonight!
Girls: Thin spooks,
Boys: Fat spooks,
Group 1: Feather-in-a-hat spooks,
Girls: Big spooks,

Boys: Wee spooks,
Group 2: Funny-as-can-be spooks,
Girls: Laugh spooks,
Boys: Scare spooks,
Group 3: Even purple-hair spooks.
All: Pull the shades! Light the light!
　　　All the spooks are out tonight!

Heaven Chant

If you want to get to heaven, let me tell you what to do.
　　(Four steps into circle.)
Just grease your feet in mutton stew.
　　(Make two circles with knees.)
And slide right out of that slippery sand.
　　(Step, slide twice.)
And ooze on over to the Promised Land.
　　(Turn around twice.)
Yeah!
　　(Raise arms in the air.)

Variation: Add instruments to accompany the chant and movement.
Line 1: Finger cymbals and triangles, 4 beats.
Line 2: Tone blocks and mallets, 4 beats.
Line 3: Maracas and sand blocks, 4 beats.
Line 4: Jingles and tambourine, 4 beats.
Line 5: Cymbal and mallet, 1 beat.

The Flag I Love
by Carrie Ester Hammil

(A choral recitation for your February program)

My country has a banner,
　All blue and red and white.
I love its brave true colors,
　That gleam so clean and bright.

My flag, my gay striped banner,
　Sparkling in the sunshine.
I'd give my all to serve it,
　I love it, and it's mine.

My country has an emblem,
　That floats on land and sea
It tells the whole world always,
　America is free!

69

My flag, my gay striped emblem,
　　Red and white and lovely blue.
May children here forever
　　Protect and keep it true.

Mrs. Peter

Yes, Peter found a pumpkin
All hidden in the weeds.
He cut the orange top off
And scraped away the seeds.
They say he made a house then
By carving out a door
And putting in a window
Or maybe three or four
And spreading out a handkerchief
To cover up the floor,
And next he put the lid on
To make it waterproof.
The stem became a chimney
That rose up from the roof,
But it was Mrs. Peter
Who busy as a gnome
Put curtains up and knicknacks
And made it look like home.

Tapping

Tapping, tapping goes the cobbler,
There's his shop across the way.
Tapping, tapping goes his hammer,
I can hear it all the day.
Tapping, tapping when I ask him,
"Please, sir, will you mend my shoes?"
Tapping, tapping while he answers,
"Surely, any time you choose."

Pigeons

My pigeon house I open wide
And I set all my pigeons free.
They fly to the tops of the tallest house
And they rest on the limb of a tree.
And when they return from their weary climb,
They fold their wings and they say "good night,
Coo-roo, coo-roo, coo-roo, coo-roo."

Five Little Chickadees

Five little chickadees
Peeping at the door,
One flew away,

And then there were four.
Four little chickadees
Sitting on a tree,
One flew away,

And then there were three.
Three little chickadees
Looking at you,
One flew away,

And then there were two.
Two little chickadees
Sitting in the sun,
One flew away,

And then there was one.
One little chickadee
Left all alone,

One flew away,
And then there were none.

The Special Night

Group 1: At last has come the night of Halloween,
Group 2: The strangest night that you have ever seen.
Group 1: Fierce dragons run along the street
Group 2: As cats and bats fall in retreat.

Chorus: Tonight, the special night, is just for spooks!

Group 1: The witches sail across the deep black sky;
Group 2: On brooms they mount and fly away up high.
Group 1: And pumpkins sit with silly grins,
Group 2: And some have teeth and some have chins.

Chorus: Tonight, the special night, is just for spooks!

Group 1: And in the shadows lurk the eerie sounds
Group 2: Of goblins making now their midnight rounds
Group 1: And pirates from the forty seas
Group 2: Come sailing in upon the breeze.

Chorus: Tonight, the special night, is just for spooks!

Group 1: On Halloween the children have fun;
Group 2: They ring doorbells and then they run.
Group 1: The people laugh because they know
Group 2: The spooky spooks just love it so.

Chorus: Tonight, the special night, is just for spooks!

The Bells
by Adelyn Jackson Richards

Long ago and far away
Bells rang out that Christmas day,
Proclaiming loud a Savior's birth,
Good will to men and peace on earth.

Once again what joy there'll be
When bells announce the world is free.
When wars with all their horrors cease,
And reigns on earth eternal peace!

The Months
Adapted from Mother Goose

(Type: Line-A-Child)

1st Child: January brings the snow;
                See the snowmen in a row.
2nd Child: February days are longer;
                Nights are cold and winds are stronger.
3rd Child: March brings breezes loud that shake
                The little flowers to make them wake.
4th Child: April brings both sun and rain
                To make the whole world green again.
5th Child: May brings songs of bird and bee,
                Joy for you and joy for me.
6th Child: June brings buttercups and roses;
                See her hands all filled with posies.
7th Child: Hot July brings cooling showers
                For thirsty fields and trees and flowers.
8th Child: August days are full of heat;
                Then fruits grow ripe for us to eat.
9th Child: September brings the goldenrod
                And milkweed flying from its pod.
10th Child: In October, nuts are brown
                And yellow leaves fall slowly down.
11th Child: November brings the chilly rain,
                Whirling winds, frosty again.
12th Child: Cold December ends the year
                With Christmas tree and Christmas cheer.

Mice*
by Rose Tyleman

All: I think mice
        Are rather nice.
Solo (1):   Their tails are long,
Solo (2):   Their faces small,
Solo (3):   They haven't any
        Chins at all.
Solo (4):   Their ears are pink,
Solo (5):   Their teeth are white,
Solo (6):   They run about
        The house at night.

*From *Fifty-one New Nursery Rhymes;* Copyright 1931 by Doubleday & Co., Inc., New York. Reprinted by permission of the publishers and The Society of Authors, London, as literary representatives of the estate of the author.

Solo (7): They nibble things
          They shouldn't touch,
Solo (8): And no one seems
          To like them much.
All: But I think mice
     Are nice.

Mrs. Peck-Pigeon
(Unison or a combination)

Mrs. Peck-Pigeon
Is picking for bread,
Bob-bob-bob
Goes her little round head.
Tame as a pussycat
In the street,
Step-step-step
Go her little red feet.
With her little red feet
And her little round head,
Mrs. Peck-Pigeon
Goes picking for bread.

Pussies on the Willow Tree

Little pussies woke up early
On our willow tree,
Fastened on the branches
Tight as they can be.

Looking down the street they saw
A gray pussycat,
And they wondered why it was
They could not walk like that?

Make Friends with Books
by Nona Keen Duffy

Make friends with books
Wherever you go;
They're good to have
And fun to know.

They've traveled far
In many lands,
In boats and ships
And caravans.

They'll tell you things
Of far and near;
New sights you'll see,
Strange tales you'll hear!

Each book you read
Befriends and stays,
To charm and gladden
All your days!

Dance of the Months

The New Year comes in with a shout and laughter
And see, twelve months are following after!
First, January all in white
And February short and bright.

See breezy March go tearing round,
But tearful April makes no sound.
May brings a pole with flower crowned,
And June strews roses on the ground.

A pop! A bang! July comes in.
Says August, "What a dreadful din!"
September brings her golden sheaves.
October waves her pretty leaves.

While pale November waits to see,
December brings the Christmas tree.
They join hands to make a ring,
And as they dance, they merrily sing:

"Twelve months are we, you see us here.
We make a circle of the year.
We dance and sing, and children hear,
We wish you all a glad New Year!"

Fairy Umbrellas

Out in the waving meadow grass
The pretty daisies grow.
I love to see their golden eyes,
Their petals white as snow.

I wonder if the fairies use
The dainty little flowers
To keep their frocks from getting wet
In sudden April showers.

Open, Shut Them

Open, shut them, open, shut them,
Give them a little clap.
Open, shut them, open, shut them,
Lay them in your lap.
Creep them, creep them,
Creep them, creep them,
Right up to your chin.
Open up your little mouth,
But do not put them in.
Open, shut them, open, shut them,
To your shoulder fly.
Then like little birdies
Let them flutter to the sky.
Falling, falling, falling, falling,
Almost to the ground.
Quickly pick them up again,
And turn them round and round.
Faster, faster, faster, faster,
Slower, slower, slower, slower.
Clap.

Part V
Finger Plays

Introduction

Objectives

The children will gain in visual skills, motor skills, attention span, understanding of drama, the order of numbers, and concepts (such as differences between left and right), language ability, and creativity.

Benefits

- Poetic fun
- Fine motor development
- Coordination of words and movement
- Sequence
- Memory and attending factors
- Rhythm and action
- Eye-hand coordination
- Tactile and kinesthetic awareness of shape and location
- Social skills
- Language development
- Coordination of action and words
- Auditory skills and auditory memory
- Feeling of self-worth

Children have always loved acting out stories and rhymes. Finger plays were once called "mother play" because they were used by mothers to amuse and comfort their children. It is also fun to develop some of your own variations on this well-loved teacher-child learning experience.

The value of finger plays is as follows: children participate in activities and learn to retain attention span, and the play rivets attention needed for dramatic expression (even on primitive levels) and to stimulate learning. Friedrich Froebel, Father of the kindergarten (1782–1852), said, "What the child imitates, he (she) begins to understand. Let him represent the flying of birds, and he enters partially into the life of birds. Let him imitate the rapid motion of fishes in the water, and his sympathy with fishes is quickened. Let him reflect in his play with varied aspects of life, and his thoughts will begin to grapple with their significance."

Finger plays mean learning through play. It is not always necessary for the child to sing the songs and do the finger plays at the same time. The teacher can improvise, embellish, and change to fit particular circumstances or needs.

An oral activity that is particularly suitable for work with primary children is the finger play story, which may aim at teaching some concept, such as the difference between left and right or the order of the numerals, in addition to encouraging young children to speak. "Five Little Chickadees" (p. 71) is an example of finger play that teaches children to count while they are developing language abilities.

A favorite finger play is "Eency, Weency Spider" (p. 92), which is a song that has appeal for children. Children can also invent finger plays to accompany familiar songs, for example, "Three Blind Mice."

The Activities

Counting Finger Plays

With two hands and fingers, count to ten.
One to ten! Then back again!
Counting with fingers can be fun.
Let's play a game! We'll start with one!

Hold up two hands. Count with fingers. One to ten, then ten to one.

Here is Susie! Here is Fred!
Next comes Sally! Then comes Ted!
Hello, Billy! Hello, Jim!
Come in Betty! Come in, Tim!
Welcome, Mary! Welcome, Arty!
I'm so glad you all came to my birthday
    party!

Starting with thumb, raise each finger, one by one, to count friends.

Come to the table! Each take a chair.
Look! A cake! Count the candles there!
One-two-three-four-five! And one more to
    grow!
Huff and puff and blow, blow, blow!

Hold up ten fingers. Bend one by one.
Count with fingers.
Blow on candle fingers. Fold down one by one.

Happy Hands

Hands up high *(raise arms above head)*
Hands down low *(bend body and dangle arms)*
Hide those hands *(put hands behind back)*
Now where did they go? *(look around you)*
Out comes one *(bring one hand in front of your face)*
Now there's two *(bring out the other hand)*
Clap them *(close hands)*
Now we're through *(drop arms to sides)*

Fun for Halloween

Peter bought a pumpkin
At the corner store,
(Form a "pumpkin" with both hands, fingers touching.)
A perfect, posing pumpkin
To place outside the door.
(Place the pumpkin on the floor.)
Peter cut a puckered mouth,
(With index finger of right hand, outline a mouth in front of own mouth.)
Then a nose quite wide.
(Outline a triangular nose.)
The eyes were round and "goggley"
(Make circles with thumb and index finger of both hands and hold before the eyes.)
For a candle light inside.
Now the pumpkin's ready
To place upon the sill.
(Place the pumpkin on the floor again.)
A welcome to the tricksters,
For one and all a thrill.
(Clap hands for applause.)
The last ghost said, "I'll have Halloween fun."
(Hold up one finger.)
Away he dashed, and then there were none.
(Put fist behind back.)

Five Little Girls

Five little girls woke up in their beds.
(Curl fingers of one hand loosely in palm.)
This little girl jumped right out bed.
This little girl shook her curly head.
(Starting with thumb, let each finger pop up for one girl.)
This little girl washed her sleepy face.
This little girl got all her clothes in place.
This little girl put on her shoes and socks.
And they all ran down to breakfast
When the time was eight o'clock.
(All fingers behind back.)

The Ball

Here's a ball for Baby
Big and soft and round.
Here's the baby's hammer
Oh, how he can pound.

Here's the baby's music
Clapping, clapping so!
Here are Baby's soldiers
Standing in a row.
Here's the baby's trumpet
Toot, toot, toot, toot, toot.
And here's the way the baby
Plays at Peek-a-boo.
Here's the big umbrella
Keeps the baby dry.
And here's the baby's cradle
Rock-a-baby-bye.

Smile Song

I've something in my pocket,
It belongs across my face,
And I keep it very close at hand
In a most convenient place.
I'm sure you couldn't guess it
If you guessed a long, long while,
So I'll take it out and put it on,
It's a great big [name of school] smile!

The Circus

Going to the circus to have a lot of fun,   *(Hold up closed fists.)*
The animals parading, one by one.   *Raise fingers to indicate each new number.)*
Now they're walking two by two,
A great big lion and a caribou.
Now they're walking three by three,
The elephants and the chimpanzee.
Now they're walking four by four,
A striped tiger and a big old bear.
Now they're walking five by five,
Make you laugh when they arrive.
Now they're walking six by six,
Little dogs jump over sticks.
Now they're walking seven by seven,
Zebras stamping on the Deven.
Now they're walking eight by eight,
Running and jumping over the gate.
Now they're walking nine by nine,
Scary rabbit and the porcupine.
Now they're walking ten by ten,
Ready to start all over again.

Jack-O'-Lanterns

Five little jack-o'-lanterns sitting on a gate.   *(Hold up five fingers.)*
The first one said, "Oh my, it's getting late."   *Point to each finger in turn.)*
The second one said, "Let's have some fun."
The third one said, "Let's run, let's run."
The fourth one said, "Let's dance, let's
    prance."
The fifth one said, "Now it's our chance."
Then "Who-o-o' went the wind, and out went   *(Blow hard.)*
    the light,   *(Run fingers behind back.)*
And away went the jack-o'-lanterns on
    Halloween night.

My Toothbrush

I have a little toothbrush.   *(Use pointer finger for toothbrush.)*
I hold it very tight.   *(Make a tight fist.)*
I brush my teeth each morning   *(Move hand up and down in brushing*
And then again at night.   *motion.)*

Ten Little Fingers

I have ten little fingers,   *(Hold up both hands showing the ten*
And they all belong to me.   *fingers.)*
I can make them do things.
Would you like to see?
I can shut them tight,   *(Put hands together tightly.)*
Open them wide.   *(Open hands wide.)*
I can hold them in front   *(Hold hands in front—stretched out.)*
Or make them hide.
I can hold hands high,   *(Hold hand over head.)*
I can put them down low,   *(Put hands low, bending slightly.)*
I can hide them in back,   *(Put hands behind you.)*
Then hold them like so.   *(Put hands in lap.)*

Here Is a Bunny

Here is a bunny with ears so funny;   *(Two fingers up straight.)*
Here is his hole in the ground;   *(Make circle of forefinger and thumb.)*

Up go his ears, and he runs to his hole,
When he hears a strange little sound.   *(Clap hands.)*

Snowflakes

Merry little snowflakes
Falling through the air,   *(Fingers raised high, moving quickly.)*
Resting on the steeple   *(Make steeple with two pointed fingers*
And the tall trees everywhere,   *and raise arms for branches.)*
Covering roofs and fences,   *(Use two hands to form a roof, then clasp*
Capping every post,   *hands together.)*
Covering the hillside
Where we like to coast.   *(Make a scooping motion of coasting.)*
Merry little snowflakes
Do their very best   *(Fingers raised high, moving quickly.)*
To make a soft, white blanket
So buds and flowers may rest.   *(Put palms together at side of face,*
                                                  sleeping motion.)

But when the bright spring sunshine
Says it's come to stay,   *(Make a circle with arms for the sun.)*
Then those little snowflakes
Quickly run away!   *(Children can quickly hide hands behind*
                                                  their backs or quickly scoot back to
                                                  their seats.)

I Have Two Eyes to See With

I have two eyes to see with,   *(Point to eyes.)*
I have two feet to run,   *(Point to feet.)*
I have two hands to wave with   *(Wave hands.)*
And a nose I have but one.   *(Point to nose.)*
I have two ears to hear with   *(Point to ears.)*
And a tongue to say good day   *(Point to tongue.)*
And two red cheeks for you to kiss,   *(Point to cheeks.)*
And now I'll run away.   *(Run away.)*

Two Little Eyes

(Point to eyes.)

Two little eyes that open and close,
Two little ears,
And one little nose,
Two little cheeks,
And one little chin,
Two little lips with teeth closed in!

(Point to ears.)

(Point to nose.)

(Point to cheeks.)

(Point to chin.)

(Point to lips.)

This Is the Church

This is the church,

And this is the steeple,

Open the door

And see all the people!

87

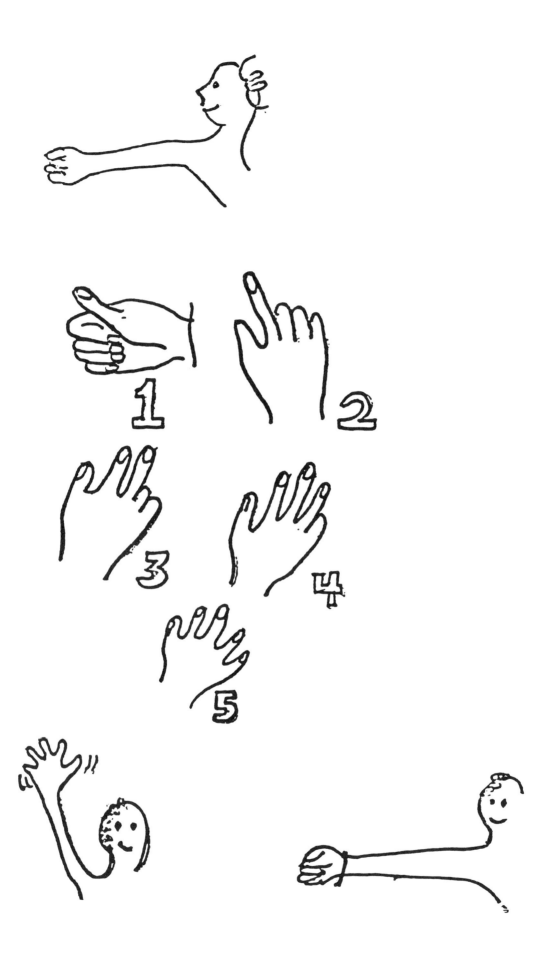

Bees

Here is a beehive   *(Make a fist.)*
Where are the bees?   *(Hold out the hand, palms up.)*
Hidden away where nobody sees.
Soon they'll be coming out of the hive.
One, two, three, four, five.   *(Make fingers come up as the counting is
                                                 done.)*

The Apple Tree

Way up in the apple tree
Two little apples smiled at me.
I shook that tree as hard as I could,
Down fell the apples,
M-m-m, were they good!

The Hand
(Thumb is Father, et cetera.)

This is Father,
This is Mother,
This is Brother tall,
This is Sister,
This is Baby,
Oh, how we love them all!

(Make cradle motions and sing a lullaby.)

Mr. Turtle

Here's Mr. Turtle,
He creeps on the ground,
With his head stuck out,
Looking all around.
If an enemy comes,
Then all is not well.
He pulls back in,
Leaving just his hard shell.

(Make fist with knuckles upward.)
(Creep fingers forward.)
*(Extend forefinger, waving it from side to
    side.)*
(Move other hand forward.)

*(Bring fingers in suddenly
making fist—knock knuckles
with other hand.)*

My Family

In my house you will see
A very happy family.
There's Daddy
And there's Mother;
There's Sister,
And there's Brother.
And who can this one be?
This little one is—me!
I'm happy as can be
God made my family.

(Hold hands together to form a house.)

(Point to thumb on left hand.)
(Point to forefinger on left hand.)
(Point to middle finger on left hand.)
(Point to ring finger on left hand.)
(Point to little finger on left hand.)
(Point to self.)

91

The Eency, Weency Spider

Eency, weency spider
Climbed up the water spout;
Down came the rain
And washed the spider out;
Out came the sun
And dried up all the rain;
Eency, weency spider
Climbed up the spout again.

(With the tip of your right forefinger touching the left thumb, twist your hands so that the left forefinger touches the right thumb and so on, making them climb up above your head in half-circles. At "down came the rain" let your arms fall. At "washed the spider out" part your hands with a sweep. At "out came the sun" raise your arms above your head and make an arch, raising them again at "dried up all the rain." The game ends by repeating the climbing movement as the spider climbs "up the spout again.")

I'm a Little Teapot

I'm a little teapot, round and stout.
(Stand up with hands by side.)
Here is my handle.
(Place left hand on left side to make a semicircle.)
Here is my spout.
(Raise right hand up; bend elbow to show spout.)
When I get all steamed up, then I shout!
(Make sound with mouth.)
Tip me over and pour me out!
(Bend sideways to show spout, right hand pouring.)

The Counting Lesson

Right hand:
Here is the beehive. Where are the bees?
Hidden away where nobody sees.
Soon they come creeping out of the hive—
One!—two!—three!—four!—five!

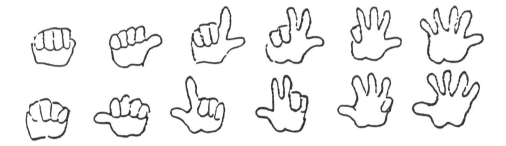

Left hand:
Once I saw an anthill
    With no ants about;
So I said, "Dear little ants,
    Won't you please come out?"
Then as if the little ants
    Had heard my call,
One!—two!—three!—four!—five came out!
    And that was all!

Part VI
Storytelling

Introduction

Objectives

The children will develop listening skills, memory, language skills, poise, speech, and the ability to retrieve previously learned information.

Benefits

- Listening skills and paying attention
- Following simple directions
- Memory skills and retention
- Speech and language in connecting words
- Acting ability
- Awareness of the order and sequence of ordinary events
- Body awareness when acting out stories
- Organization of a story told in sequence, each with an action that moves the story along
- Special awareness
- Gross motor skills experience
- Auditory skills

> The storyteller refreshes the weary, rejoices the sad, and multiplies the joy of those who are already glad.
>
> —Cynthia Maus

Agnes de Mille at one time was asked to describe the effect the great dancer Pavlova had upon her pupils. She replied, "She made our lives less daily."

Any teacher can do just this for children when she has acquired the art of telling stories. It's inspiring to look into the eyes of pre-school handicapped children whose eyes tell you, "We are waiting." It may be a day of disappointment or one of sheer happiness. Whatever the day offers, a well-told story will enrich it for every child.

How does one become a good storyteller? One must first be enthusiastic about developing the art and careful in the selection of the story to fit the age (pre-school) and background of the group for which you are planning. Then, after having read the story many times, prepare, as one would string beads on a thread for a necklace. Collect materials for the story. For example, if you're telling the story about the three bears, make a chart or draw the three bears to illustrate during the time you are telling the story. You may also use a flannel board. Everything used to illustrate the story is *hands-on material* which the young child can handle, even the blind child if the bears are fuzzy and soft. Always begin the story with a good opening and continue to add items in sequence to the thread of the story until the story has been completed. And clasp it together with a well-chosen final sentence.

Say it aloud so that you may hear the effect now that you have learned to tell it. Learn to tell a few stories well and be rewarded by the enthusiastic faces in your audience. Always speak clearly and loud enough for the hard-of-hearing child.

An old principal in describing a successful teacher said, "She has the outward sign of inward warmth." This also describes the face of a storyteller who is thoroughly enjoying the story with her audience.

Rudyard Kipling is said to have inveighed against the way history was taught in schools. He felt history should be told in story form and then children would never forget it.

There is something contagious about storytelling. If children see that the storyteller is thoroughly enjoying it, they will go to the library to seek out more story collections. May Lamberton Becker once told a group of librarians that the effect of well-chosen and narrated stories is like measles going through an orphanage.

The value of storytelling lies in children's ability to:

1. Dramatize and role play.
2. Retell stories through art.
3. Store away descriptive words and phrases to appear later in their conversation.
4. Create stories or put new endings on old stories such as: Cinderella did not lose her slipper, but —————————.

The greatest value of storytelling for a teacher is the fact that it is a painless process of teaching. A good storyteller may age outwardly, but a core of childhood remains.

Here are some stories guaranteed to make the reader anxious to become a good story-teller.

The Stories

Key

Heavy lines indicate where to fold.

Dotted lines indicate the "before" position of the paper.

Solid lines indicate the "after" position of the paper.

Jagged lines indicate where the paper is to be ripped.

Step One

Take four full length sheets of newspaper.

Step Two

Fold all sheets in half, as one.

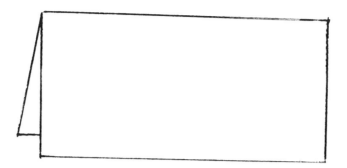

Step Three

Fold top edges over to meet at the center of the paper to form flaps Y and Z and points A, B, and C. Note: The shape of a triangle is formed.

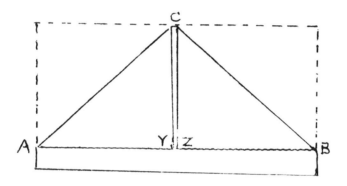

Step Four

At the bottom of the paper, fold four sheets of paper upwards to meet the bottom of flaps Y and Z. Fold strip up again. Do the same on the other side. The shape is used as the sailor's hat and his boat.

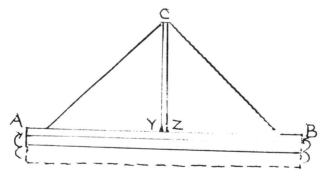

Step Five:

Pull the boat open from the center and fold Point A down to Point B. Note: This will form the shape of a square; open to boat to continue story.

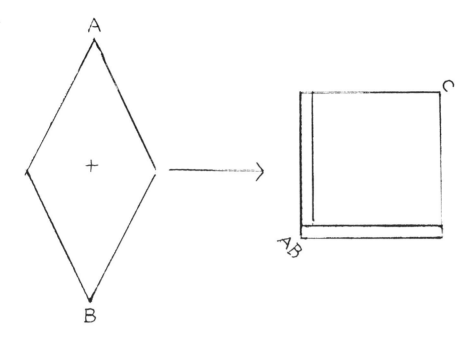

Step Six

Rip Point B off for front bow hitting an iceberg.

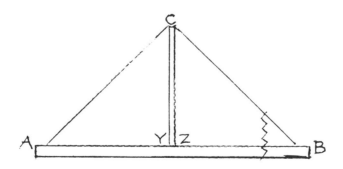

Step Seven

Rip Point A off for the rear stern hitting another iceberg.

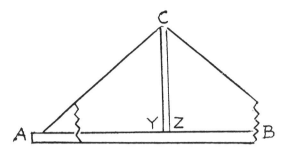

Step Eight

Rip Point C off for strong winds . . . that rip the sails off.

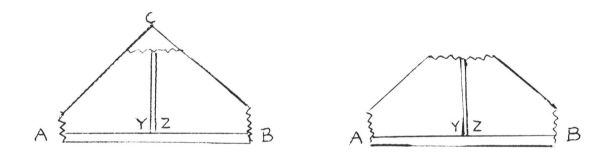

Step Nine

Sailor's shirt is made by unfolding the bottom of the ship and unfolding flaps Y and Z.

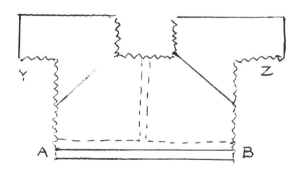

The Three Little Pigs

Once upon a time, there was an old sow with three little pigs, and as she was poor and had not enough to keep them, she sent them out to seek their fortune.

The first that went off met a man with a bundle of straw and said to him, "Please, man, give me that straw to build me a house." The man did, and the little pig built a house with it.

Presently, along came a wolf and knocked at the door and said, "Little pig, little pig, let me come in."

To which the pig answered, "No, no, by the hair of my chinny-chin-chin."

"Then I'll huff, and I'll puff, and I'll blow your house in," said the wolf.

So he huffed, and he puffed, and he blew the house in and ate up the little pig.

The second little pig met a man with a bundle of sticks and said, "Please, man, give me those sticks to build a house." The man did, and the pig built his house.

Then along came the wolf and said, "Little pig, little pig, let me come in."

"No, no, by the hair of my chinny-chin-chin."

"Then I'll huff, and I'll puff, and I'll blow your house in."

So the wolf huffed, and he puffed, and he puffed and he huffed, and at last he blew the house in, and he ate up the little pig.

The third little pig met a man with a load of bricks and said, "Please, man, give me those bricks to build a house with." The man gave him the bricks, and he built his house with them.

The wolf came, as he had to the other little pigs, and said, "Little pig, little pig, let me come in."

"No, no, by the hair of my chinny-chin-chin."

"Then I'll huff, and I'll puff, and I'll blow your house in."

Well, he huffed, and he puffed, and he huffed, and he puffed, and he puffed, and he huffed, but he could not blow the house in. When he found that, with all his huffing and puffing, he could not blow the house in, he said, "Little pig, I know where there is a nice field of turnips."

"Where?" said the little pig.

"Oh, in Mr. Smith's field, and if you will be ready tomorrow morning, I will call for you, and we will go together and get some for dinner."

"Very well," said the little pig. "I will be ready. What time do you plan to go?"

"At six o'clock," said the wolf.

Well, the little pig got up at five and got the turnips before the wolf came.

When the wolf came at six o'clock, he said, "Little pig, are you ready?"

The little pig said, "Ready! I have been there and come back again and got a nice potful for dinner."

The wolf felt very angry at this, but he thought that he could fool the little pig somehow or other, so he said, "Little pig, I know where there is a nice apple tree."

"Where?" said the pig.

"Down at Merry-garden," replied the wolf, "and if you will not deceive me, I will come for you at five o'clock tomorrow, and we will go together and get some apples."

Well, the little pig bustled up the next morning at four o'clock and went off for the apples, hoping to get back before the wolf came. But he had farther to go, and he had to climb the tree, so that just as he was climbing down from it, he saw the wolf coming, which, as you may suppose, frightened him very much.

When the wolf came up, he said, "What, little pig! Are you here before me? Are they nice apples?"

"Yes, very," said the little pig. "I will throw you down one." And he threw it so far that, while the wolf was gone to pick it up, the little pig jumped down and ran home.

The next day the wolf came again and said to the little pig, "Little pig, there is a fair at Shanklin this afternoon. Will you go?"

"Oh, yes," said the pig, "I will go. What time shall you be ready?"

"At three," said the wolf.

So the little pig went off before the time, as usual, and got to the fair and bought a butter churn. He was going home with it when he saw the wolf coming. Then he did not know what to do.

So he got into the churn to hide and, in doing so, turned it round, and it rolled down the hill with the pig in it. This frightened the wolf so much that he ran home without going to the fair.

He went to the little pig's house and told him how frightened he had been by a great round thing that come down the hill past him.

Then the little pig said, "Hah, I frightened you, did I! I had been to the fair and bought a butter churn, and when I saw you, I got into it and rolled down the hill."

Then the wolf was very angry indeed and declared he would eat up the little pig and that he would climb down the chimney after him right now.

When the little pig saw what the wolf was about, he hung up a pot full of water and lit a blazing fire. Just as the wolf was coming down, he took off the cover, and in fell the wolf. The little pig put on the cover again in an instant, boiled him up, and ate him for supper and lived happy ever afterwards.

The Three Bears

Once upon a time, there lived three bears. Papa Bear was big and growly. Mamma Bear was middle-sized and pleasant. And Baby Bear, well, he was small, and sometimes—he squeaked!

They lived in a pretty little house. Papa Bear pounded nails in the roof. Mamma Bear watered the flowers. Baby Bear did tricks on the lawn. They were very happy.

One day Mamma Bear made some fine porridge. "It smells good!" she said.

"It looks good!" said Baby Bear.

"But it's too hot," finished Papa Bear. "Let's take a walk while it cools." And away they went.

Pretty soon a little girl came down the path. Her name was Goldilocks, because her hair was like sunshine. "I wonder who lives here," she thought. "I think I'll stop to visit."

She went inside, and there was the porridge on the table. "It looks so good," she said to herself, "I'm going to try it."

That is just what Goldilocks did. But she found that the porridge in Father Bear's big bowl was much too hot. And Mamma Bear's middle-sized bowl was too cold. So—

She tried Baby Bear's tiny bowl. And, do you know, it was just right! Goldilocks ate it all!

"Now," she thought, "I'll sit down and wait for the people to come home."

First she sat in Papa Bear's big chair, but that was too hard.

Then she tried Mamma Bear's middle-sized chair, but that was so soft she could hardly climb out of it.

Last of all, she tried Baby Bear's tiny chair. It was just right!

Goldilocks sat down happily.

But Baby Bear's chair was very small. Goldilocks had been sitting in it for only a minute when—CRASH! Down it fell and broke to pieces.

Goldilocks tried to make the little chair stand up again. Then she saw the staircase, and quick as a wink, she ran up the steps to see what she could see.

There was Papa Bear's big, wide bed. Goldilocks lay down on it, but it was too hard. Then she tried Mamma Bear's middle-sized bed, but that was so soft she could hardly see up over the quilts. Last of all, she tried Baby Bear's tiny bed. Do you know, it was just right!

It felt so good that Goldilocks went to sleep. And while she slept, the three bears came home.

Papa Bear went right to his big bowl. "Someone," he growled, "has been tasting my porridge.

"And look here," said Papa Bear. "Someone has been sitting in my big chair."

"And in my middle-sized chair," said Mamma Bear.

"Oh," squeaked Baby Bear. "Someone has broken my tiny chair all to pieces!"

With a very loud squeak, "Someone's been lying on my bed, and she's still here!"

Just then Goldilocks woke up. She saw the three bears standing there beside the bed.

Well, with one jump she was at the top of the stairs. And with another jump she was downstairs, running just as fast as she could.

"Come back," called the three bears. "We want to be friends."

But Goldilocks kept on running. And it was a long, long time before she went walking that way again.

Little Red Riding Hood

Once upon a time, in a cottage on the edge of the wood there lived a pretty little girl. She always wore a red hood when she went visiting, and so she was known to everyone as Little Red Riding Hood.

One afternoon Little Red Riding Hood's mother called to her. "Will you take this basket of cookies and tea cakes to Grandma?" she said. "She isn't feeling well today."

"Oh, yes, Mother!" said Little Red Riding Hood, for she loved to visit her grandmother. She ran to get her little red hood.

Her mother tied the hood under Little Red Riding Hood's chin. "Promise that you won't stray off the path," she said.

Little Red Riding Hood promised and started off into the woods.

She stopped to say hello to her old friends Mr. and Mrs. Squirrel and gave them some cookies.

She looked in on the Bunny family—there were three new babies.

And at last she paused to take a drink from the bubbly brook.

She was picking wildflowers for her grandmother when suddenly she heard a voice. "Good day, Red Riding Hood," said the voice. "What are you doing here in the woods?"

Little Red Riding Hood looked up. Standing nearby was a great big wolf!

Little Red Riding Hood shivered. But then she saw that the wolf was smiling. Certainly he couldn't mean to harm her!

"I'm on my way to Grandma's house with this basket of cookies and tea cakes," she said bravely. "She isn't feeling well today."

"Hm-m-m!" said the wolf. "And where does your grandmother live?"

Little Red Riding Hood was surprised. She thought everyone knew that! "Why," she said, "she lives in the cottage by the waterfall."

"Ah, yes," said the wolf, "that cottage! I'll have to drop in to say hello one of these days."

Little Red Riding Hood bid the wolf good-day and hurried on her way to see her grandmother.

The wolf waited until she was out of sight. Then he scurried through the woods, using a path that only he knew about.

Soon he came to the cottage beside the waterfall. He knocked at the door.

"Who is there?" called Grandma.

"It's Little Red Riding Hood," called the wolf in a tiny voice.

"Why, just lift the latch and walk in, dear," answered Grandma.

When Grandma saw the wolf, she screamed and leaped right out of bed. Through the back door she ran, with the wolf close behind her.

Little Red Riding Hood opened the door and entered Grandma's cottage. She stopped and her eyes grew round when she saw the wolf snuggled down in her grandmother's bed.

"Goodness gracious, Grandmother," she said. "What big eyes you have!"

"The better to see you with, my dear," answered the wolf.

"And, Grandma," said Red Riding Hood, "what very long, long ears you have!"

"The better to hear you with, my dear," answered the wolf.

"And, Grandma," said Red Riding Hood, going a bit nearer, "what great, huge teeth you have!"

"The better to eat you with, my dear," growled the wolf. And he jumped out of bed.

But just then the door burst open. Little Red Riding Hood's grandmother came running in, and with her was a big strong woodsman carrying his ax.

"There!" cried Grandma, pointing at the wolf. "There he is!"

The wolf was frightened when he saw the woodsman. He ran around the table and around the stove and out the open door, with the woodsman right behind him. The last Little Red Riding Hood saw of him, the wolf was racing away down the path, trying not to trip on Grandma's nightgown.

The Elephant on the Bus
by Rube Rosen

The blue bus stopped at the corner. A man got off and an elephant got on. The bus driver looked at the elephant and said, "My goodness, you can't ride on my bus!"

The elephant said, "But I must get back to the zoo for lunch. I have money for the fare." And he extended his trunk with the money in it.

The driver said, "But . . . but . . . you still can't ride on my bus. You're too big!"

The elephant looked very unhappy. He said, "But I'm only a small elephant. I won't take up much room. I'll make myself real small."

The people on the bus told the driver to let the elephant come into the bus, and finally the driver said, "Well, all right. You can ride on my bus, but you may not take up more than one seat."

So the elephant paid his fare and sat down. He scroonched himself together, rolled up his long trunk, and sat as still as he possibly could. He sat so still he didn't even move his eyes.

At the next corner a lady got on and sat in the seat in front of the elephant. She was wearing a red hat with a long, long feather that curved back over the seat and touched the elephant's trunk.

108

As the bus rode along, the feather jiggled up and down, and this tickled the poor elephant's trunk. The elephant felt like sneezing. He wanted to turn away, but he was afraid he would bump the man sitting next to him. He wanted to speak to the lady about the feather in her hat, but he would have to unroll his trunk to speak, and there wasn't enough room for that.

The feather kept jiggling up and down, up and down, and tickled him more and more. He felt . . . he felt . . . hanh . . . hanh. He felt . . . he felt . . . hanh . . . hanh . . . HANH . . . CHOOOO!

It was a tremendous sneeze. His scroonched-up body spread out like a balloon, and his rolled-up trunk spanned straight out, and he sneezed the hats right off the people on the bus.

The red hat with the long, long feather landed on the driver's head, and the driver's cap landed on the elephant's head. All the hats in the bus flew off and landed on different heads. Everyone looked very silly.

The driver stopped the bus, and all the people passed around hats until they all had their own back again. Then the driver told the elephant he would have to get off the bus. All the people decided it would be the best thing to do. So the elephant got off the bus and walked back to the zoo.

On the way he had another big sneeze, right out in the open, so nobody's hat was blown off.

And from that day on, you never see an elephant on a bus.

The Mice Who Lived in a Shoe
by Rodney Peppe

This is a story about a shoe . . .
and the family of mice who lived in it.
Ma, Pa, Grandpa, Grandma, Tim, Ann, Mick, Sue, Mary, Pip.

When it rained, they got wet.
When it snowed, they got cold.
When the sun shone, they got hot.
When the wind blew, they flew all over the place.

But the worst thing of all
was when the cat put his paw
into the shoe and stretched out his claws.
The family huddled together at the toe end for safety. They all
squeaked until the cat went away.

When they were sure the cat had gone,
they gathered round Ma in the dark.
"The only way to be safe from the cat
and to shelter from the weather," said Pa,
"is to build a house."

"Where, where?" the family cried.
"Right here, in this shoe," replied Pa.
"What a good idea," said Ma,
"I'll make the curtains."
"There'll be other things to do before that,"
observed Grandpa.

Pa asked everyone to draw their dream house.

There was a big house, a small house,
a short house, a tall house, a fat house,
a thin house, a long house, a red house,
a blue house and a green house.

Pa looked at them carefully
to see who had the best ideas.
Then he drew their dream house.

The next day, a junk merchant came
to take away all their broken furniture.
Pa didn't get much money for it,
but it was enough to buy tools and materials.

They started to build the house.

Grandma gave the orders.
Pa sawed the timber.
May held the ladder.

Pa helped Ann to mix cement.
Ma held the shoe string for Mick to cut.

Sue sawed the roof timbers.
Mary fetched bricks for Grandpa.

Ann made a play platform.
Mary and Tim made the windows and doors.

Mick made the balcony.
Pip made the tea.

Their relatives came from across the valley.
Their friends came too.

Pa and Sue were working on the roof.
The others were inside, hanging the curtains.

Pa, Ma and their family were overjoyed
to have such lovely things for their new home.
They thanked their friends and relatives
and offered them some tea.

"We heard you were building a house,"
said Uncle Jack.

"So we've brought you some furniture,"
added Aunt Jane.

The last pieces were moved in.
Soon it would be time for bed.

Everyone admired the house.

Sue and Pip served the tea.

When the sun shone, they kept cool.
And when the wind blew, they stayed safe inside.

But the best thing of all
was when the cat came to put his paw
into the shoe to stretch out his claws . . .
he couldn't!
For where there was once a hole,
there was now a house!

Bear Goes Shopping

Bear like to shop a little every day. What does he buy? See if you can guess.
It's Monday. Bear is going to the bakery. What will he buy? See if you can guess.

It's Tuesday. Bear is going to the pet store. What will he buy? See if you can guess.

It's Wednesday. Bear is going to the grocery store. What will he buy? See if you can guess.

It's Thursday. Bear is going to the bookstore. What will he buy? See if you can guess.

It's Friday. Bear is going to the hardware store. What will he buy? See if you can guess.

On Saturday Bear works in the yard planting, cutting, watering and digging. And on Sunday he rests.
Take it easy, Bear-Bear.

The Bear's Bike
by Emile W. McLeon

Every afternoon we go bike riding. I check the tires and the brakes and make sure the handlebars turn. Then I get on my bike and coast down the driveway. I look to the right and to the left. I make the hand signal for a right turn, and I turn right. If I have to cross the street, I stop and get off my bike. I look both ways. If no cars are coming, I walk my bike across the street. I watch for car doors that are open. I steer around cans and broken glass. I stop for dogs to make sure they are friendly. When I meet another biker, I stay to the right. And when I come up behind people, I warn them so they can get out of the way. When I go down a hill, I don't go too fast and I use my brakes. I always start home before it is dark and put away my bike. I wipe my feet before going in the house. Then we have milk and crackers.

Mr. and Mrs. Pig's Evening Out

Once upon a time, there lived a family of pigs. There was Father Pig and Mother Pig. And then there were ten piglets. They were called Sorrell Pig, Bryony Pig, Hilary Pig, Sarah Pig, Cindy Pig, Toby Pig, Alon Pig, William Pig, Garth Pig and Benjamin Pig.

One evening mother pig called the children to her, and they were playing all over the house. "Now piglets," she said, "your father and I are going out this evening."

There was a chorus of groans. "Not far," said Mrs. Pig, "and I've asked a very nice lady to come and look after you."

"What is her name?" asked William Pig.

"I don't like baby sitters," said Benjamin.

"Oh," said Mrs. Pig, looking vague. "Well, she's coming from the agency so I'm not sure what her name is, but you're sure to like her."

"We didn't like the last one from the agency," grumbled Garth.

"I'm sure you'll find that this baby sitter will be very nice. Now get along into your bath, and I'll come and tuck you in before we go out."

The piglets took so long as they could having their baths and made a great many puddles and splashes in the bathroom, but at last mother pig got them upstairs.

Just as she was putting on her best dress, the front door bell rang. Down ran Mrs. Pig, grunting and puffing in her haste, to open the door.

A dark face peered at her, heavily wrapped in a macintosh and hat. "Are you Mrs. Pig?" asked a gruff voice.

"Yes," said mother pig brightly. "Do come in. The children are just getting into their

114

beds. They sleep in bunk beds," she explained, and so they did. Two to a bed, head to tail, stacked five beds high.

"Can you help me?" called father pig from the bedroom.

Mrs. Pig hurried upstairs. He was just putting on his smart shirt which he always wore when they went out. It was dark blue, and Mrs. Pig liked him to wear it because she thought it made him look thinner.

Unfortunately, the buttons would keep coming undone, so that everyone always noticed how very tight the shirt had become. Mrs. Pig struggled to get it done up. Suddenly, she remembered that she had not asked the baby sitter's name. She ran out of the bedroom again. The baby sitter was just settling herself comfortably on the sofa.

"Would you mind telling me what you are called?" said Mrs. Pig. "The children do like to know."

"It's Mrs. Wolf," said the baby sitter, crossing a pair of dark hairy legs and getting out her knitting.

"Oh, thanks," said Mrs. Pig, without thinking. "Now, Mrs. Wolf, I've left the kitchen light on, and if you should feel like making yourself a hot drink or having something to eat later in the evening, do please help yourself."

"Thank you, I shall," said Mrs. Wolf.

At that moment, Mr. Pig called through to say that he was quite ready, and with many farewell kisses and hugs for the children, Mr. and Mrs. Pig went out for the evening with light hearts. Mrs. Wolf sat in the living room and read magazines and knitted. The piglets all seemed to have gone to sleep—she went upstairs once to check. It seemed a very long evening. There was nothing to watch on TV. After a while, Mrs. Wolf began to feel empty, so she went into the kitchen. But she didn't turn on the kettle; no, she turned on the oven. Then she tiptoed up to the piglets' bedroom. In the lowest bunk bed were Garth and Benjamin snoring faintly. Mrs. Wolf looked longingly at Garth, all rosy, plump and pink. Then she snatched him up and carried him off downstairs. He made such a snorting and squealing that all his brothers and sisters sat bolt upright in bed. Whatever was going on? Quick as a flash, Sorrel cried, "After him, everyone, Mrs. Wolf is not be to trusted." Seizing Garth's blanket off his bed, the nine piglets galloped downstairs as fast as their short legs would carry them. They were in the nick of time. Mrs. Wolf was bending over the oven with her back to them, holding Garth, about to put him in. "Four of you take this side of the blanket," hissed Sorrel outside the kitchen. The piglets did as they were told. "Now!" ordered Sorrel. They ran in and threw the blanket over Mrs. Wolf's head. She backed away from the oven still holding Garth. Muffled snarls came through the blanket. The piglets held on tight. Mrs. Wolf struggled and thrashed, but she could not get out. She dropped Garth and went down on all fours. Garth wriggled free. The piglets hung on. Mrs. Wolf braced herself and humped her back, her long hairy tail lashing from side to side. Terrible growls came from her. "Hang on, everyone!" shouted Sorrel. Mrs. Wolf leapt into the air. The piglets were tossed to and fro, but still they hung on bravely. As soon as they were back on their feet, they circled round her so that the blanket was wrapped tighter and tighter.

Then they tied the four corners together so that she could not possibly get out and left her in the middle of the kitchen. When their father and mother came home, the ten piglets told them what a narrow escape they had had.

Father pig went out into the night and carried the blanket bundle to the middle of the bridge. There he leaned over the parapet and shook Mrs. Wolf into the swirling depths of the big river. And she was not heard of again for a very long time.

The Blind Men and the Elephant

Long ago in India, six blind men lived together. Because they lived in India, they often heard about elephants. But because they were blind, they had never seen an elephant. The blind men lived near the palace of a rajah. The rajah was the ruler of all the people. At the palace of the rajah, there were many elephants. "Let us go to the palace of the rajah," said one blind man. "Yes, let us go," said the others. It was a hot day, but the six blind men walked to the palace. They walked, one behind the other. The smallest blind man was the leader. The second blind man put his hand on the shoulder of the leader. Each blind man put his hand on the shoulder of the man in front. A friend of the six blind men met them at the palace. An elephant was standing in the courtyard. The six blind men touched the elephant with their hands. The first blind man put out his hand and touched the side of the elephant. "How smooth! An elephant is like a wall." The second blind man put out his hand and touched the trunk of the elephant. "How round! An elephant is like a snake." The third man put out his hand and touched the tusk of the elephant. "How sharp! An elephant is like a spear." The fourth blind man put out his hand and touched the leg of the elephant. "How tall! An elephant is like a tree." The fifth blind man reached out his hand and touched the ear of the elephant. "How wide! An elephant is like a fan." The sixth blind man put out his hand and touched the tail of the elephant. "How thin! An elephant is like a rope."

The friend of the six blind men led them into a garden. The six blind men were tired. It was a hot day. "Wait here. I shall bring you water to drink." They sat down in the shade of a big tree.

"You must not go out in the sun until you rest," he said.

The six blind men talked about the elephant.

"An elephant is like a wall," said the first blind man.

"A wall!" asked the second blind man. "You're wrong. An elephant is like a snake."

"A snake?" said the third blind man. "You're wrong. An elephant is like a spear."

"A spear?" said the fourth blind man. "You're wrong. An elephant is like a tree."

116

"A tree?" said the fifth blind man. "You're wrong. An elephant is like a fan."
"A fan?" said the sixth blind man. "You're wrong. An elephant is like a rope."
The six blind men could not agree. Each man shouted.

"A wall!"   "A tree!"
"A snake!"   "A fan!"
"A spear!"   "A rope!"

The friend of the six blind men came back with water to drink. At the same time, the rajah was awakened by the shouting. He looked out and saw the six blind men below him in the courtyard. "Stop!" called out the rajah. The six blind men stopped shouting. They knew that the rajah was a wise man. They listened to him. The rajah spoke in a kind voice. "The elephant is a big animal. Each man touched only one part. You must put all the parts together to find out what an elephant is really like."

The six blind men listened. They drank the cool water as they rested in the shade. They talked quietly. "The rajah is right. Each one of us knows only a part. To find out the whole truth, we must put all the parts together." The six blind men walked out of the courtyard. The smallest blind man led the way. The second blind man put his hand on the shoulder of the leader. Each blind man put his hand on the shoulder of the man in front. They walked home, one behind the other.

Cheer Up, Pig!
by Nancy Jewell

"I feel good," said Pig,
staring at a patch of sunlight on the barn floor.
"I'm so happy, I can't wait to tell somebody!"
Pig ran outside.
"Where is everybody?" he called. "It's me, Pig!"
No one answered.
"Oh, well," said Pig, "I'm here anyway."
Then he had an awful thought.
Maybe everyone was hiding.

"This is silly.
I'm just feeling sorry for myself," he said.
"Feel happy again, Pig!"
Pig waved his curly tail.
"I said, feel happy, Pig!" he shouted.
Pig rolled over in the mud.
Pig rolled over again.
"I love mud!" said Pig.
"So why does it feel so cold and awful?
I must be hungry."

Pig stuck his head in his trough.
"This food has no taste.
Maybe I'm not taking big enough bites.
It's no use.
I don't feel like eating alone.
I don't feel like doing anything alone."

Pig heard happy shouts coming from the woods.
"Oh, no!" he cried.
"I bet all my friends are playing a game together,
and they forgot to ask me!
I'll go to sleep,
then I won't feel lonely."

Pig shut his eyes
and lay very still.
"Think of nothing, Pig," he said.
The wind rattled the branches of the maple tree.
A tractor cranked loudly.
"It's too noisy to sleep!"
Pig tried again.

"Think of floating, Pig.
You are a feather.
You are a feather drifting along on the wind."
Pig sighed, almost asleep.
"Now you are drifting gently over the pond," he whispered.
Pig rolled over in his sleep.

"UGH!" he yelled, opening his eyes.
He was lying in a big puddle of water.
"You're not a feather, Pig,
you're just a pig."
Pig lay on the ground, too sad to get up.
"I know! I'll tell myself jokes.
Then I'll feel good again.
Knock, knock," said Pig.
"Who's there?" answered Pig.
But nobody was there.

"I GIVE UP!" shouted Pig.
"How can I tell jokes by myself?"
Pig stared at the big maple tree.
"I wish I was a tree.
Trees never feel lonely."
Pig signed.
"I am going to cry," he said.
"That is the one thing I can do by myself."

Pig lay down on his back.
He sniffed a little sniff.
Then he sniffed a big, loud sniff.
A bird chirped loudly overhead.
"It's so noisy," said Pig.
"I can't even hear myself cry!"
He looked up at the maple tree.

Mama Robin was perched beside her nest on a high-up branch.
Suddenly, three little robins hopped out of the nest.
Mama Robin flew in a little circle around the branch and back.
The first little robin did the same thing.
So did the second little robin.
"Pig," whispered Pig,
"can you believe you are seeing three baby birds
getting their first flying lesson?"

The third little bird stood on the branch and didn't move.
"Come on, baby bird!" shouted Pig.
The little robin flapped its tiny wings.
Then it, too, flew once around the branch and back.
"I knew you could do it!" shouted Pig.

Pig did a little dance on his hind legs.
A silver dandelion puff floated by Pig, tickling his nose.
"I wonder where you're going,"
said Pig, chasing after the puff ball.
It floated right over his trough.
"Have a good trip, puff," called Pig, stopping to eat.
"Food, you don't taste half bad.
Hmmm!" Pig plunged his whole head into the trough.

Then he went over to his mud and rolled over.
"Mud, now you are beginning to feel nice and muddy."
"Pig!" someone called.
Pig didn't answer.
He wanted the someone to go away
so he could keep rolling in the mud.
"Pig!" someone shouted.
"Who's that?" said Pig crossly.
"It's me," said Duck.

"What are you doing, Pig?"
"Rolling in my mud."
"Aren't you lonely?" asked Duck.
"No," said Pig, standing up.
"How can you have fun all by yourself?" asked Duck.
"It's easy," said Pig.
"But since you are here,
I will tell you a joke."

"Say, 'Knock, knock,' Duck."
"Knock, knock," said Duck.
"Who's there?" said Pig.
"I don't know," said Duck, looking around.
"You are silly!" said Pig.
Duck and Pig laughed so hard
they both fell down in the mud.

"Ick," said Duck.
"I'm going to my pond to take a bath."
"I'll see you later," said Pig.
"I'm taking my bath in the mud."
Duck left.

"I'm glad I'm not a feather.
I'm a pig!" said Pig happily,
as he rolled over and over in the mud.

The Town Mouse and the Country Mouse

Once a contented country mouse had the honor of receiving a visit from his old friend who lived at His Majesty's Court. The country mouse was extremely glad to see his guest and very hospitably set before him the best cheese and bacon, young wheat and corn which his cottage afforded. As for their beverage, it was the purest water from the spring. After supper, the two sat by the open hearth and chatted. "Really my good friend," said the town mouse, "I am amazed that you can keep up your spirits in such a dismal place and with such rustic fare to eat. Truly, you are wasting your time here. Why, at court there is dancing and feasting and all kinds of merriment. In short, there never is a humdrum moment. But you must return with me tomorrow and see for yourself!" The country mouse decided to sleep on

it and told his guest he would give him his answer the next morning. Then they retired in peace and quietness for a good night's rest.

The next morning when the guest was ready to journey back to town, he urged his friend to accompany him to His Majesty's Court: "Such pomp and elegance and cuisine ought not to be missed." The country mouse finally consented to go along, so the two friends set out together. It was late in the afternoon when they arrived at His Majesty's Court, and there, in the great dining hall, they found the remains of a sumptuous dinner. There were creams and jellies and sweetmeats, all of the most delicate kind. The cheese was the finest Parmesan, and they wetted their whiskers with exquisite champagne. But before they had half finished their delightful repast, they were greatly alarmed by the barking and scratching of a dog. Then, the meowing of a cat almost frightened them to death. And a whole army of servants burst into the room and cleared everything away in an instant.

The two mouse was by this time safe in his hole—which, by the way, he had not been thoughtful enough to show his friend. Why, the poor country mouse could find no better shelter than that afforded by the round leg of a sofa. There he waited in fear and trembling till quietness was again restored. "Oh! My dear friend," said the country mouse as soon as he recovered enough to have the courage to speak, "if your fine living is interrupted constantly with fear and danger, let me return to my plain food and my peaceful cottage. For what good is elegance without ease, or plenty with an aching heart?"

The town mouse asked his friend to stay and spend the night. But the country mouse said, "No, no. I have seen enough of the Court life; I shall be off as fast as I can."

And he ran out into the night . . . and did not stop until he reached the peace and quiet of his cottage.

Eighteen Cousins

I went for a visit; I went to a farm.
I went to my cousins' when it was warm.
I went to my cousins' (whom I'd never seen).
I counted my cousins—and I counted eighteen!

I looked at a horse down on the farm.
I looked at a pig out by the barn.
I looked at a cow (and it was a she).
I looked at a lamb—but what did I see?
EIGHTEEN cousins a-looking at me!

I watched baby chick scratch on the ground.
I watched baby ducklings waddle around.
I watched a new gosling peck at a tree.
I watched an old rooster—but what did I see?
EIGHTEEN cousins a-watching me!

I sniffed at the sky; I sniffed at the air.
I sniffed at the flowers that grew everywhere.
I sniffed dandelions that grew close to me,
That grew by my feet—like a big yellow sea.
I sniffed and I sniffed—but what did I see?
EIGHTEEN cousins a-sniffing like me.

I took off my shoes (I knew I must),
And I walked in the garden in the soft brown dust.
I walked through the grass as high as my knee.
I walked a little faster—but what did I see?
EIGHTEEN cousins a-walking with me!

I nibbled a carrot; I nibbled a pea.
I nibbled a green leaf—but what did I see?
EIGHTEEN cousins a-nibbling like me!

I jumped on a stone; I jumped on the grass.
I jumped on a stick and broke it in half.
I jumped over steps (I think there were three).
I jumped up and down—but what did I see?
EIGHTEEN cousins a-jumping after me!

I ran down the lane; I ran through the woods.
I ran to the meadows as fast as I could.
As fast as I could and as fast as could be.
I ran like the wind—but what did I see?
EIGHTEEN cousins a-running after me.

I chased a bobwhite back to his nest.
I chased a rabbit, who had stopped to rest.
I chased a butterfly, and I chased a bee.
I chased a grasshopper—but what did I see?
EIGHTEEN cousins a-chasing me!

I came to a brook; I had to stop,
But a frog splashed in with a big ker-plop.
Up came the snails in the little green brook.
Up came a fish to take a good look.
Up came a beetle, up came a flea,
Up came a glider—but what did I see?
EIGHTEEN cousins a-coming close to me.

I tried to hide, but I fell on my knee.
I fell in the tall grass and couldn't get free.
I tugged and I tugged—but what did I see?
EIGHTEEN cousins, and they caught me!

We laughed out loud and we laughed out long.
We laughed and we laughed till we laughed a song.
We laughed because it's fun to be
EIGHTEEN cousins—And One Little Me!!!

A Treeful of Pigs

One day a farmer and his wife went to market. They saw some pigs that were for sale.
"Such good round pigs," said the farmer. "We must buy them."
"What a lot of work it will be to raise these pigs," said the farmer's wife.
"It will not be hard. We will do it together," said the farmer.
The farmer and his wife bought the pigs and brought them home to their farm. The next day the farmer's wife came to the farmer and said, "My dear, you must help me plant the corn so our pigs will have something to eat." Now, the farmer was a very lazy man. He liked to spend most of his time lying in bed, asleep with his head on the pillow.
The farmer said, "If you will plant the corn today, I will help you another day."
"But when?" asked the farmer's wife.
"On the day that pigs bloom in the garden like flowers. On that day I will help you plant the corn," said the farmer.
In the morning when the farmer woke up, he looked out of the window. He saw that pigs were blooming in the garden like flowers. But he put his head back down on the pillow and went to sleep. "What a lazy husband I have!" said the farmer's wife, and she planted the corn herself.
Soon after, the farmer's wife came to the farmer and said, "My dear, you must help me dig a hole and fill it with mud so that our pigs will have a cool place to sit."
The farmer said, "If you will dig the hole today, I will help you another time."
"But when?" asked the farmer's wife.

"On the day that pigs grow on trees like apples," said the farmer. "On that day I will help you dig the hole."

In the morning when the farmer woke up, he looked out of the window. He saw that pigs were growing in the trees like apples. But he put his head back down on the pillow and went to sleep. "What a lazy husband I have," said the farmer's wife, and she dug the hole and filled it with mud.

By and by, the farmer's wife came to the farmer and said, "My dear, you must help me carry buckets from the well so our pigs will have fresh water."

The farmer said, "If you will carry the buckets today, I will help you another time."

"But when?" asked the farmer's wife.

"On the day that pigs fall out of the sky like rain. On that day I will help you carry buckets of water," said the farmer.

In the morning when the farmer woke up, he looked out of the window. He saw that pigs were falling out of the sky like rain, but he put his head back down on the pillow and went to sleep. "What a lazy, lazy husband I have," said the farmer's wife, and she carried the buckets of water from the well herself.

When the corn was ripe, the farmer's wife came to the farmer and said, "My dear, you must help me harvest the corn so our pigs will have a fine dinner."

But the farmer yawned and said, "I wish the day would come when those pigs would disappear like the snow in the spring. On that day I will really rest well."

In the morning when the farmer woke up, he looked out of the window. He did not see the pigs anywhere. They were not blooming in the garden like flowers. They were not growing on trees like apples. They were not falling out of the sky like rain. They had disappeared like the snow in the spring.

124

"What have I done?" cried the farmer. "What has happened to our wonderful pigs?" The farmer called his wife to his bedside. "My dear," said the farmer, "you must help me look for our lost pigs."

The farmer's wife said, "If you will look for them today, I will help you another time."

"But when?" asked the farmer.

"On the day that you jump out of bed, put on your clothes and promise never to be lazy again," said the farmer's wife. "On that day, I will help you look for our lost pigs."

The farmer quickly jumped out of bed. He put on his shirt and pants and his boots. He fell on his knees and cried, "I will never, never be lazy again!"

"Good enough," said the farmer's wife. The farmer's wife ran outside and opened the cellar door. All the pigs came bouncing out into the sunshine.

The farmer helped his wife harvest the corn. He helped her cook the meal. Then the farmer, the farmer's wife and the pigs sat down to a delicious dinner of corn pudding and hot corn muffins on the day the farmer promised always to keep his promise—and from that day on, he did.

Two Greedy Bears

Two bear cubs went out to see the world. They walked and walked, till they came to a brook.

"I'm thirsty," said one.

"I'm thirsty," said the other.

They put their heads down to the water and drank.

"You had more," cried one and drank some more.

"Now you had more," cried the other and drank some more.

And so they drank and drank, and their stomachs got bigger and bigger, till a frog peeked out of the water and laughed. "Look at those pot-bellied bear cubs! If they drink any more, they'll burst." The bear cubs sat down on the grass and looked at their stomachs.

"I have a stomach-ache," one cried.

"I have a bigger one," cried the other.

They cried and cried till they fell asleep.

In the morning, they woke up feeling better and continued their journey.

"I'm hungry," said the one.

"I'm hungrier," cried the other.

And suddenly they saw a big round cheese lying by the roadside. They wanted to divide it. But they did not know how to break it into equal parts. Each was afraid the other would get the bigger piece. They argued, and they growled, and they began to fight, till a fox came by.

"What are you arguing about?" the sly one asked the bear cubs.

"We don't know how to divide the cheese so that we'll both get equal parts."

"That's easy," she said. "I'll help you." She took the cheese and broke it in two.

But she made sure that one piece was bigger than the other, and the bear cubs cried, "That one is bigger!"

"Don't worry. I know what to do." And she took a big bite out of the larger piece.

"Now that one's bigger!"

"Have patience." and she took a big bit out of the second piece.

"Now this one's bigger."

"Wait, wait," the fox said with her mouth full of cheese. "In just a moment they'll be equal." She took another bite and then another. And the bear cubs kept turning their black noses from the bigger piece to the smaller one, from the smaller one to the bigger one.

"Now this one's bigger!"

"Now that one is bigger!"

And the fox kept on dividing and dividing the cheese, till she could eat no more. "And now, good appetite to you, my friends!" She flicked her tail and stalked away.

By then, all that was left of the big, round cheese were two tiny crumbs. But they were equal!

The Cat and the Fiddler

One morning a fiddler walked through town with his cat trailing at his heels. Shop-keepers were beginning to open their shops. Housewives were sweeping their stoops. The milkman, with his cart, was just finishing his rounds.

"Pardon me," said the fiddler to the milkman. "I am a stranger in town. Perhaps you could direct me to a place where I might have breakfast."

The milkman smiled and reached down to pat the fiddler's cat. "Why, of course," he replied. "There is a fine place just down the street. By the way, this looks like such a fine cat. Perhaps you would sell her to me."

"Oh, I wouldn't think of selling her," replied the fiddler. "This is a very special cat."

"I would take good care of her," said the milkman. "She could catch the mice on my milk cart, and I would feed her the finest of cream."

"No," said the fiddler, smiling. "I could not part with her. Watch." With that, he picked up his fiddle, tucked it under his chin, and began to play a jig. Suddenly, the cat started to dance. First she danced on her hind paws; then she danced on her front paws. She whirled around and around, bobbing gracefully to the tune the fiddler played. Finally, the fiddler stopped. "As you can see," he said, "she is a very special cat."

By this time, of course, many people had gathered to hear the fiddler play and to watch the cat dance. Now they began to applaud wildly.

"A dancing cat is indeed special," said one of the men. "Such a fine cat should not be sold just to hunt mice. Perhaps you would sell her to me. She could perform in my carnival."

The fiddler shook his head. "Oh, no," he replied. "I do not intend to sell her at all. One

does not part with such a special cat." And with that, he put his fiddle away and walked on down the street.

Now the fiddler was in no hurry to leave the town. He played lullabies for the babies in their carriages. He played jigs for the children in the parks. He played waltzes for young people. He played airs for the old people. He played something for everyone, and as he did so, his cat would dance to the music. Everyone loved the cat and the fiddler. Never had the town's people been so happy.

One day, however, the king heard of the fiddler and his cat. "Send for them at once!" he cried. "I must see what is so special about this pair." Soon the fiddler and his cat appeared at the palace. "I want you to amuse me," ordered the king crossly.

The fiddler bowed low. The cat bowed low. "It is a privilege to perform for you, your majesty," said the fiddler. With that, he tucked his fiddle under his chin and began to play. The cat rose on her hind paws and began to dance. Together they did their best. Never had the fiddler played so well; never had the cat danced so splendidly.

When they had finished, the court began to applaud with delight. "Bravo!" they cried. "Wonderful! Magnificent! Tremendous!"

The king smiled haughtily. "Your performance was indeed well worth my time," he said. "Now, what is your price for such a dancing cat?"

"This cat is not for sale, your majesty," answered the fiddler softly. "This is a very special cat. I could never sell her to anyone because she has no price."

"So it shall be, then," stated the king. "I shall take the cat and give you nothing in return." Instantly, the cat was snatched away from the fiddler. "Be gone with you," ordered the king.

"But, your majesty," protested the fiddler, "don't you wish me to stay and play for you and the cat?"

"What nonsense!" exclaimed the king. "I have musicians who play one hundred times better than you."

"But this is a very special cat," protested the fiddler. "I am the only one who . . . " It was too late. The poor fiddler was thrown outside.

"Now then," exclaimed the king once the fiddler was gone, "let the musicians begin. I wish to see more of this dancing cat." The court musicians began to play. And the cat began to dance. One by one, everyone in the court began to tap his toes. One by one, the ladies of the court began to dance. Soon, even the king himself was dancing. The cat led the dance around and around. Finally, the king grew tired. "Enough!" he shouted. "The musicians may stop." But the musicians couldn't stop playing. "I said enough!" shouted the king. "The ladies and gentlemen may stop dancing." But the ladies and gentlemen of the court couldn't stop dancing. Even the king himself couldn't stop dancing.

"Help! Help!" cried the king. "I am tired. Cat, stop your dancing. I command you to stop!" The cat, however, was not tired. She danced faster and faster and faster. The cat danced outside the courtroom. Everyone followed, dancing. She danced down the palace steps. Everyone followed, dancing. She danced outside the palace gates. Everyone followed, dancing. Finally, she danced straight to the fiddler.

"Help us, help us!" gasped the king. "Stop your dancing cat!"

"Oh, but it's not my cat anymore," said the fiddler with a smile. "Don't you remember, your majesty? You took her from me. You stop her."

"I can't. I've tried!" cried the king. He could barely lift his feet, yet he continued to dance. "I'll give her back to you. Just make her stop dancing!"

The fiddler picked up the fiddle, tucked it under his chin, and began to play softly. Instantly, the king, the ladies and gentlemen of the court, and all the musicians fell, exhausted, to the ground. "Come, puss," said the fiddler to his cat. "We must be on our way." The fiddler continued to play, and the cat continued to dance as they walked down the road. That night, the fiddler patted his cat while she purred contentedly. "You are indeed a very special cat," said the fiddler. "And I shall never part with you." Then he poured a huge bowl of cream. Even a very special cat likes cream.

The Christmas Santa Almost Missed
by Marion Frances

It was Christmas Eve, and Santa was ready to go. Hurry! Hurry! He put on his boots. Hurry! Hurry! He put on his coat. He put on his mittens and looked for his cap. "Where's my cap?" said Santa. "Where is your cap? Where is your cap?" Santa looked under his bed and under his chair. He looked under the mat and under the cat. "Where is my cap?" said Santa. "You shall not go without your cap." "Where is my cap?" said Santa. Hurry! Hurry! He looked in his pack Where was his cap? It's getting late. It's getting late. He was ready to go. But where was his cap? "Look! Santa, look! There is your cap." Hurry! Hurry! It's getting late. Then Santa put on his cap and took his big pack—and was ready to go—on Christmas Eve.

The Monkey and the Bee

by Leland Jacobs

See! See!
What do I see?
I see a tree.
Yes, I see a tree.

See! See!
What do I see?
I see a bee.
Yes, I see a bee.

See! See!
What do I see?
I see a monkey.
I see a tree.

See! See!
Oh, what do I see?
I see a monkey.
I see a tree.

Do you see a bee?
Oh! Oh?
A tree?
A bee?

I see a monkey in the tree.
What do you see?
Yes, what do you see?
Look! Look!
What do you see?

I see the bee fly to the tree.
I see the bee on the monkey's tree.
Look in the tree.
What do you see?

I see the monkey look at the bee.
Oh! See!
What do you see?
I see the monkey hit at the bee.
Oh, the monkey hits at the bee.
Look! Look! Look at the bee.

The Little Rabbit Who Wanted Red Wings

Once upon a time, there was a little White Rabbit with two beautiful pink ears and two bright red eyes and four soft little feet—SUCH a pretty little White Rabbit, but he wasn't happy.

Just think, this little White Rabbit wanted to be somebody else instead of the nice little rabbit that he was.

When Mr. Bushy Tail, the gray squirrel, went by, the little White Rabbit would say to his Mummy, "Oh, Mummy, I wish I had a long gray tail like Mr. Bushy Tail's."

And when Mr. Porcupine went by, the little White Rabbit would say to his Mummy, "Oh, Mummy, I wish I had a back full of bristles like Mr. Porcupine's."

And when Miss Puddle-Duck went by in her two little red rubbers, the little White Rabbit would say, "Oh, Mummy, I wish I had a pair of red rubbers like Miss Puddle-Duck's."

So he went on wishing and wishing until his Mummy was quite tired out with his wishing. One day Old Mr. Ground-Hog heard him wishing.

Old Mr. Ground-Hog is very wise indeed, so he said to the little White Rabbit, "Why don't you go down to Wishing Pond, and if you look in the water at yourself and turn around three times in a circle, you will get your wish."

So the little White Rabbit trotted off, all alone by himself through the woods, until he came to a little pool of green water lying in a low tree stump, and that was the Wishing Pond. There was a little, little bird, all red, sitting on the edge of the Wishing Pond to get a drink, and as soon as the little White Rabbit saw him, he began to wish again.

"Oh, I wish I had a pair of little red wings!" he said. Just then, he looked in the Wishing Pond, and he saw his little white face. Then he turned around three times and something happened. He began to have a queer feeling in his shoulder, like he felt in his mouth when he was cutting teeth. It was his wings coming through. So he sat all day in the woods by the

131

Wishing Pond waiting for them to grow, and by and by, when it was almost sundown, he started home to see his Mummy and show her, because he had a beautiful pair of long, trailing red wings.

But by the time he reached home it was getting dark, and when he went to the hole at the foot of a big tree where he lived, his Mummy didn't know him.

No, she really and truly did not know him, because, you see, she had never seen a rabbit with red wings in all her life. And so the little White Rabbit had to go out again, because his Mummy wouldn't let him get into his own bed. He had to go out and look for some place to sleep all night.

He went and went until he came to Mr. Bushy Tail's house, and he rapped on the door and said, "Please, kind Mr. Bushy Tail, may I sleep in your house all night?"

But Mr. Bushy Tail opened his door a crack, and then he slammed it tight shut again. You see, he had never seen a rabbit with red wings in all his life.

So the little White Rabbit went on and on until he came to Miss Puddle-Duck's nest down by the marsh, and he said, "Please, kind Miss Puddle-Duck, may I sleep in your nest all night?"

But Miss Puddle-Duck poked her head up out of her nest just a little way, and then she shut her eyes and stretched her wings out so far that she covered her whole nest and said, "No, no, no, go away."

You see, she had never seen a rabbit with red wings in all her life.

So the little White Rabbit went on and on until he came to Old Mr. Ground-Hog's hole, and Old Mr. Ground-Hog let him sleep with him all night, but the hole had beechnuts spread all over it. Old Mr. Ground-Hog liked to sleep on them, but they hurt the little White Rabbit and made him very uncomfortable before morning.

When morning came, the little White Rabbit decided to try his wings and fly a little, so he climbed up on a hill and spread his wings and sailed off. But he landed in a low bush all full of prickles, and his four feet got mixed up with twigs so he couldn't get down.

"Mummy, Mummy, Mummy, come and help me!" he called.

His Mummy didn't hear him, but Old Mr. Ground-Hog did, and he came and helped the little White Rabbit out of the prickly bush.

"Don't you want your red wings?" Mr. Ground-Hog asked.

"No, NO!" said the little White Rabbit.

"Well," said the Old Ground-Hog, "why don't you go down to the Wishing Pond and wish them off again?"

So the little White Rabbit went down to the Wishing Pond, and he saw his face in it. Then he turned around three times, and sure enough, his red wings were gone.

A Surprise for Mrs. Bunny
by Charlotte Steiner

In the woods there lived eight little bunnies. Their names were: Rolly, Dolly, Trolly, Molly, Lolly, Wolly, Polly, and Jolly.

One day, one of the eight little bunnies whispered to his sisters and brothers, "Tomorrow is Mother's birthday. Let's surprise her with a birthday present."

Next morning, the eight little bunnies went over to the hens' house. Each bunny carried home a big white egg. They put them in a basket, but it still did not look like a birthday

present. The eggs were just plain everyday eggs. Little Trolly had a clever idea. "Let's paint each egg a different color," he said. So they all started out to find the color each of them liked best.

Dolly stopped to look through a nearby fence and saw a pretty flower garden, full of lovely red roses. "What color could be nicer than red," thought Dolly.

And Dolly painted her egg red like the roses.

Trolly went to visit her friend, the little pig. The kind little pig gave Trolly a bunch of carrots to eat. "My, these taste good," said Trolly, "and they are such a nice color too."

So Trolly painted his egg orange like the carrots.

Rolly met a yellow duck. "How wonderful your feathers look in the bright sunshine! Yellow is such a beautiful color," he said.

And Rolly went home and painted his egg yellow like the duck's feathers.

Molly went to a nearby vegetable garden. In this vegetable garden grew the best lettuce in the country.

Molly was very fond of lettuce, and she ate as many of the fresh green leaves as she could.

And Molly painted her egg the lovely green color of lettuce.

Wolly soon grew tired of looking for a pretty color and lay down on the grass. He looked up at the sky. "Oh, isn't the sky beautiful!" he exclaimed. "It's so blue."

And Wolly decided to paint his egg blue like the sky.

Lolly sat down to write a birthday poem for Mama Bunny. But alas! She wiggled and spilled the ink all over her egg.

So Lolly had to paint her egg black like the ink.

Poor Jolly was very sad because he was the only one who did not have a colored egg for Mama Bunny's basket. He had to put the plain white egg in the basket. Just then Mama Bunny came home.

"Surprise! Surprise!" cried all the little bunnies—all except Jolly.

Then Mrs. Bunny saw the beautiful basket. "What a lovely present!" she cried. "This is the happiest birthday I ever have had."

But that was not the whole surprise!

Just then there was a sharp, cracking sound. It was the white egg. It broke in two and out stepped a little yellow chick. "This is the most wonderful surprise of all," exclaimed Mrs. Bunny.

And the eight little bunnies thought so too.

Papa's Panda

That morning Papa came instead of Mama to wake up James, and Papa sang to him, "Happy birthday to you! Happy birthday to you!"

"Where's my present?" demanded James.

"Mama's wrapping it," said Papa.

"Is it a teddy?" asked James. "I really want a teddy bear like Danny Jackson's."

"What kind of teddy does Danny Jackson have?"

"It's brown and eats crackers," said James.

"I don't think Mama is wrapping a brown teddy that eats crackers," said Papa.

"But I want a teddy like Danny's."

"You haven't even seen your present yet," said Papa.

"I don't want to see it!" shouted James. "I won't open it!"

"Then I'll open it for you," said Papa.

"Then I'll throw it away," said James. "I want a teddy like Danny's."

"I don't know why you want a teddy that looks like somebody else's. I never even wanted a teddy when I was a boy. I wanted a panda."

"A real panda?" asked James.

"No, a toy panda. The real pandas live in China."

"Can we ever get a real panda for a pet?" asked James.

Papa shook his head. "There are not many real pandas left. If there is a keeper of pandas in China, I am sure he would not let us keep one for a pet."

"But maybe the keeper of pandas would let a panda visit us," said James.

"Oh, visit!" exclaimed Papa. "That's quite another thing. If a panda wished to visit us, the keeper might let him."

134

"How could he come?" asked James. "By airplane?"

"By airplane," said Papa. "He would come by airplane."

"And he would order some ginger ale," said James.

"No, he wouldn't," said Papa. "Pandas like bamboo. He would order juice of bamboo on ice."

"And after the juice of bamboo on ice?" asked James.

"He would drink juice of bamboo on ice until the plane landed in New York," said Papa. "And we would be there to meet him."

"Suppose we couldn't find him," said James.

"Oh, but we could," said Papa. "Pandas are big."

"How big?"

"As big as I am," said Papa.

"Suppose he doesn't fit in the car?" asked James.

"We would have to buy a bus," said Papa.

"But suppose we don't have enough money to buy a bus?" asked James.

"Why, we would all go to work. Mama would work, you would work."

"What would I work at?" asked James.

"You would run the elevator at Wallace's. And after work, we would eat our supper and go directly to bed because we'd be so tired."

"And the panda—where would he sleep?" asked James.

"With you," said Papa. "He's your panda."

"But my bed is too small!" said James.

"Then Mama and you and I would push our beds together for him," suggested Papa.

"And where would we sleep?" asked James.

"On the floor," said Papa.

"Why can't the panda sleep on the floor?"

"Why," said Papa, "Because he's the guest."

"And since he's coming from the bamboo forest, he won't have any clothes. I would have to give him my new suit."

"Do pandas wear clothes?" asked James.

Papa shook his head.

"Not in the forest. But this panda would see my new suit, which I would be wearing when I met him at the airport. And he would say, 'I WANT A SUIT. I WANT A SUIT JUST LIKE YOURS.'"

"Would it fit him?" asked James.

"No. He'd burst all the seams. This panda is very fat . . ."

". . . because he eats a lot," said James. "And he'd ask for bamboo leaves, and we wouldn't have any.

"Then he'd say, 'WHAT ELSE HAVE YOU GOT FOR A PANDA TO EAT?'"

"And then he'd open the refrigerator and eat up all the ice cream."

"And then he'd take a bottle of milk and drink in the living room, and he'd spill it on the sofa. And you would spank him," said James.

"No, I wouldn't," said Papa. "He's too big. He'd say, 'GET OFF MY SOFA!' And maybe he'd spank me."

"And would you cry?" asked James.

"I might cry," said Papa, "if he spanks me very hard."

"Don't worry, Papa. Maybe he won't come."

"Maybe he won't come till winter, anyway," said Papa. "That will give us all time to learn Chinese."

"Why do we have to learn Chinese?"

"So we can talk to the panda."

"Is Chinese hard to learn?"

"For me, yes," said Papa. "I am sure it will be hard for me."

"We'll have to learn it fast," said James, "because he might be on his way right now. And he'll march up to the front door and knock three times."

"And Mama and I will hide under the bed," said Papa, "and you will answer the door."

"Why do I have to answer the door?"

"Because this panda listens to children but not grown-ups. So when you open the door, you must say to him very gently, 'I am sorry that I already have a panda.' "

"But I don't have a panda," exclaimed James. "I DON'T HAVE A PANDA!"

At that moment, Mama put her head in the door of James' room.

"What's all the yelling about?" she asked.

"I need a panda," said James. "I need one right away."

"It just so happens," said Mama, "that you have a panda."

And she handed James a box wrapped in red paper. He tore off the paper and lifted the lid of the box. There lay a panda. A little one.

The Search

Once upon a time, far back in the woods lived a very busy woman and her little boy, Robbie. The woman said to the little boy, "Please go into the woods and fetch me some firewood to keep us warm. Also, I'd like you to look for a little red house without windows or doors, but it has 'Star Lights' inside."

The little boy started on his way, and suddenly, he decided to take his little friend along whose name was Nancy. They walked and walked and walked.

They ran into a little old lady. The little boy said to the little old lady, "Miss, have you seen a red house without windows or doors, but it has 'Star Lights' inside?"

The little old lady said, "No, no, my son, I haven't. If I had, I would live in it to keep warm."

The two children walked on, and they met a little old man. They said to the little old man, "Sir, have you see a red house without windows or doors, but it has red 'Star Lights' inside?"

"No, no," said the little old man. "My children, I have terrible headaches, pains in my ears and rheumatism, and if I see a house like that, I would live in it. That's fine to have a house like that."

The two children walked and walked and walked. A terrible wind and rain storm came up, and they found themselves in the middle of a terrible rain storm, and in the orchard fruit was falling all over. A huge apple fell from the tree. It hit the little boy directly on the head. He picked it, and, always wanting to share with friends, he reached for his knife and cut the apple in half, using the long part of the apple and cutting it across the long way with the knife. When cut this way, the "Star Lights" will be seen directly.

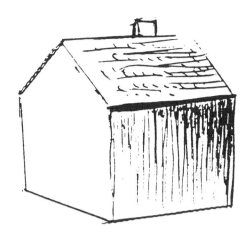

Ophelia
by Alice Meeker

This is a Halloween story. Ophelia is a witch with a green face, yellow broom, black dress and pointed black hat. Soon it gets late, and it is over. Mrs. Doby carries Ophelia to the attic to wait for next Halloween. Each time Mrs. Doby goes to the attic, she explains the symbol of the next holiday. After many trips, Mrs. Doby brings Ophelia down to the garden to enjoy the Halloween with her companion, Pumpkin Boy. There Ophelia enjoys sitting and visiting with the children and Pumpkin Boy.

The Three Wishes

Once upon a time, and to be sure it was a long time ago, there lived a poor woodsman in a great forest, and every day of his life he went out to cut timber. So, one day he started out, and the good wife filled his wallet and slung his bottle on his back, that he might have meat and drink in the forest. He had marked out a huge old oak, which, he thought, would furnish many and many a good plank. And when he came to it, he took his axe in his hand and swung it round his head as though he were of a mind to fell the tree at one stroke. But he hadn't given one blow when what should he hear but the most pitiful entreating, and there stood before him a fairy who prayed and beseeched him to spare the tree. He was dazed, as you may fancy, with wonderment and affright, and he couldn't open his mouth to utter a word.

But he found his tongue at last. "Well," said he, "I'll even do as thou wishest."

"You've done better for yourself than you know," answered the fairy, "and to show I'm not ungrateful, I'll grant you your next three wishes, be they what they may."

And there, with the fairy no more to be seen, the woodsman slung his wallet over his shoulder and his bottle at his side, and off he started home. But the way was long, and the poor man was regularly dazed with the wonderful thing that had befallen him. When he got home, there was nothing in his noodle but the wish to sit down and rest. Maybe, too, it was a trick of the fairy's. Who can tell?

Anyhow, down he sat by the blazing fire, and as he sat, he felt hungry, though it was a long way off to suppertime. "Hast thou naught for supper, dame?" said he to his wife.

"Nay, not for a couple of hours yet," said she.

"Ah!" groaned the woodsman. "I wish I'd a good link of black pudding here before me." No sooner had he said the word, when chatter, chatter, rustle, rustle, what should come down the chimney but a link of the finest pudding the heart of man could wish for.

If the woodman stared, the good wife stared three times as much. "What's all this?" said she.

Then all the morning's work came back to the woodsman, and he told his tale right out, from beginning to end.

As he told it, the good wife glowered and glowered. When he had made an end of it, she burst out, "Thou bee'st but a fool, Jan, thou bee'st but a fool, and I wish the pudding were at thy nose, I do, indeed." And before you could say Jack Robinson, there the good man sat, and his nose was the longest for a noble link of black pudding. He gave a pull, but it stuck; she gave a pull, but it stuck; and they both pulled till they had nigh pulled the nose off, but it stuck and stuck.

"What's to be done now?" said he.

"T'isn't so very unsightly," said she, looking hard at him.

Then the woodsman saw that if he wished, he must need a wish in a hurry, and wish he did that the black pudding would come off his nose.

Well! There it lay in a dish on the table, and if the good man and the good wife didn't ride in a golden coach or dress in silk and satin, why, they had at least as fine a black pudding for their supper as the heart of man could desire.